GIN
CAKE &
RUCKSACKS

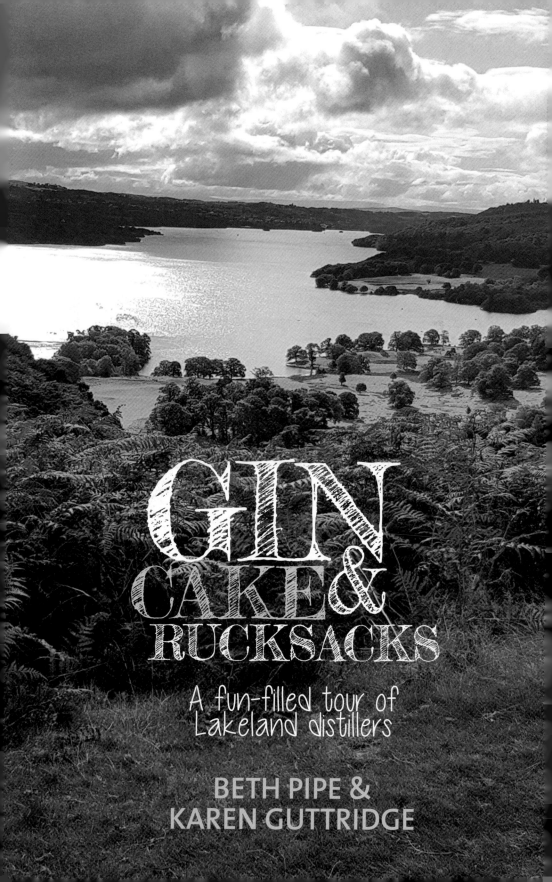

GIN
CAKE &
RUCKSACKS

A fun-filled tour of Lakeland distillers

BETH PIPE &
KAREN GUTTRIDGE

The route

This is a trail, not necessarily a hike, so for each segment of the route we've provided directions for those travelling by train, bus, bike, car (please don't drink and drive), and on foot. All landmarks mentioned are taken from the OS maps for the region. Train routes are given where they exist, but as bus routes change regularly your best bet is to check local timetables for up-to-date information.

If you do choose to hike this route please be aware that some terrain may be challenging and refer to the www.mountain.rescue.org.uk for safety advice.

First published in 2018
by Palatine Books,
Carnegie House,
Chatsworth Road
Lancaster LA1 4SL
www.palatinebooks.com

The right of Beth Pipe and Karen Guttridge to be identified as the authors of this work has been asserted in accordance with the Copyright, Designs and Patents act 1988

British Library Cataloguing-in-Publication data
A catalogue record for this book is available from the British Library

Paperback ISBN 13: 978-1-910837-17-7

Designed and typeset by Carnegie Book Production
www.carnegiebookproduction.com

Printed and bound by Cambrian Press

TOG (The Outdoor Guide) is a free online resource set up by Julia Bradbury to provide outdoor information for walks all around the UK. www.theoutdoorguide.co.uk

Contents

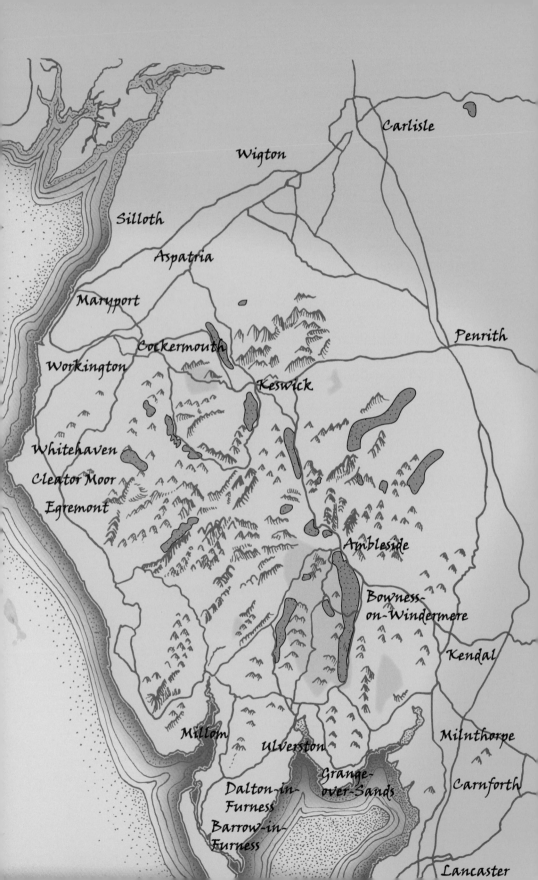

How it all started…

SOMETIMES IT'S HARD TO pin down exactly when a project began. Many simply evolve over time, but we can put an absolute date on the start of this one: April 9th 2017. 9:58 a.m. to be precise. Having known each other via social media for several years, in 2016 myself and Karen, both being mad about writing and a little old fashioned, decided to become penpals – there really is nothing quite like receiving a nice handwritten letter in amongst the pile of bills and junk mail.

The previous day I'd received a letter from Karen in which she'd foolishly said, "I really fancy doing some sort of challenging/quirky walk and writing about it (hopefully humorously) so if you have any ideas, send them over!"

As luck would have it I had indeed had an idea for a "challenging/ quirky" walk and I knew it would be right up Karen's street. I didn't have chance to contact her that day but the next morning I sent her a message via Facebook:

> As it happens I do have an idea that may suit us, though it's a Cumbrian walk. There are loads of distilleries in Cumbria now and I was thinking of creating a walking book called 'The Spirit Guide' which connects them all. A sort of long-distance pub crawl. I was pondering how to do it myself but if you're looking for something different I'd be up for hiking it together.

Thankfully Karen was completely up for it, which is how the whole 'Two-women-who've-never-met-united-by-a-love-of-gin-forge-a-new-long-distance-footpath' idea came to be.

Over the following months we hammered out a schedule and a route, all via email and messenger, sharing our ideas and concerns – at this point we'd still never actually spoken (even as I type that I realise how crazy it sounds) and really knew very little about each other. To rectify this we decided to exchange a number of frank emails ahead of our adventure, in an attempt to fill in some of the blanks and let each other know just what they were getting into. Reading them back now, they may have done more harm than good…

17th August, 11:45

Dear Karen

Well, the start of the adventure is nearly upon us so I thought it wise to share a little more information, seeing as how we've never met and will be sharing a room on our first night together.

First off I should let you know that a few other friends are a little concerned about the fact that we only know each other via social media, and one of them in particular is concerned that in reality you could be a 20-stone biker named Barry from Milton Keynes. I've tried to put their mind at ease by explaining that 'Barry' probably wouldn't have gone to the trouble of writing 4 books to maintain his persona but I've promised to keep Steve (my husband) handy, just in case, please don't take this personally. Of course it could be me that's Barry... Anyway, some things you should probably know about me. Firstly, I notice that from your social media posts you appear to be a little more refined than I am. My idea of packing for a 12-night hike involves 12 clean pairs of undies, a few clean t-shirts, couple of pairs of socks and maybe a clean bra if we're really pushing it. I think Steve is hoping I might pick up some good habits from you.

Whilst I don't smell (at least no-one has ever mentioned it) I keep personal grooming to a bare minimum as frankly I find it boring, and there are so many other things I could be doing instead (did you know the average person spends over 60 hours a year in the shower?). Oh, and because my hair takes around 2 days to dry, it gets washed twice a week max.

I am also concerned about the fact that I snore, so you may want to pack ear plugs.

Assuming none of that has put you off, I'm really looking forward to our hike – I think it will be a fantastic adventure and I can't wait to get stuck in!

Big love

Beth

17th August, 15:54

Okay well first off... I'm still coming!

I died laughing that my social media persona appears refined – I *was* once called 'posh bird' (only cos I declined karaoke) and someone told me I talk 'very BBC', but he was from Newcastle. You're definitely more refined than me; I will be taking only 6 pairs of knickers and rinsing through.

Some of my friends have been totally freaking out about this trip we have planned. WHAT? YOU'VE NEVER MET??!! So you'll either be indoctrinating me into a cult, you're a serial killer or we are going dogging throughout genteel Cumbria.

Right, assuming we both survive the first meeting, here are a few things you might be better off knowing.

If there is a fan in the room and we use it, I will hear voices. No accounting for what they tell me to do. Fan noise = weird Gregorian chanting.

If there are cupboards in the room, I can't sleep until the doors are closed. Why, you say? WHY?? Everyone knows that if you don't shut the doors, the bogey man comes out and gets you!

If you have eggs for breakfast and split the yolks so that vile yellow goo pools everywhere, I will be sick.

I wear sunglasses. A lot. Probably even in Cumbria. (Knackered one eye with a tennis ball and it's a bit light sensitive.) So I *will* probably look like someone capable of kneecapping you.

There must be more but I'll ease you in gently.

Still coming?

Love Barry

18th August, 11:15

Dear Barry/Karen

I am SO with you on the cupboards thing and would only add that they should all be thoroughly checked first – I can't sleep in a strange hotel room without first ensuring there is nothing untoward hiding in any of the cupboards.

Eggs may be a problem as I adore them, but am willing to forgo them for the sake of the friendship – would scrambled be okay or are they best just banished? (Makes mental note to sneak into local chippy and demand pickled eggs for the rucksack.)

While we're on the subject of food, I eat anything – and I mean *anything*. Well, maybe not quite, but the only foods on my 'no' list are cottage cheese, wallpaper paste and raw celery. Other than that I recommend guarding your food closely.

Hiking wise you should know I'm very slow and very easily distracted in a 'right, let's crack on and get this done, oooohhh look at the pretty flower' kind of a way. I'm also stubborn – if the map says there is a path then there should be a path, and I will attempt to walk over or through whatever may be blocking our way. Be prepared to rescue me from 6ft-high nettles, barbed wire fences or fields of frisky bullocks.

I'm also not very good with other people getting too close – you know, the sorts of people who, in an empty restaurant, will sit right next to you, park within inches of you in an empty car park or have the temerity to want to walk the same path at the same time as we do. But I want to assure you that I will deal with all such inconveniences in a properly adult British fashion – I will tut loudly, say nothing and shake my head imperceptibly. Should said people notice any of this and ask if there is a problem I will, of course, tell them that there is not.

I know we've never met but, from the things you post on social media, we seem to share the exact same sense of humour and a love of gin and liqueurs, so whatever happens on this hike I know we'll end up laughing about it. We'll also probably end up hiking with hangovers more than we anticipated, so we'll probably both be wearing dark glasses whatever the weather.

Big love

Beth

18th August, 16:47

I also eat anything. Except eggs, obviously. I would eat wallpaper paste rather than eggs. If you want me to chow down on eggs, hide them in cakes. Of course I don't expect my breakfast companions to forego eggs on my behalf. My husband eats eggs every day, bless him. He just comes and drags me from the toilet cubicle when he's finished.

I like hiking slow. I will battle with nettles and barbed wire on your behalf but you're on your own with the frisky bullocks. While we're talking wildlife (well, almost) you are in charge of spiders. I will also jump on you, piggyback style, if a dog comes hurtling our way.

I see you don't like other people barging into your comfort zone. How many paces behind do you want me to walk?

I'm pretty sure we'll get along fine. Yes it's a bit weird I guess having never met and heading off for 10 days or so and sleeping together (ahem) the first night, but there's free gin involved so what can you do?

We will laugh a whole lot and make it fun.

My biggest worry is that my alcohol tolerance seems to have plummeted. I'll be drunk after two and well hungover the next day.

Bazza x

PS I'll put some practice in this week sitting near people eating scrambled eggs. I can do this. If there are runny bits, I cannot do this.

21st August, 18:40

Five paces behind should just about do it. And separate tables for breakfast. Kidding. Though I am a lot quieter than my social media image may suggest, so if I go all quiet on you please don't be alarmed; I promise I won't necessarily be plotting your downfall or anything. Honest.

While we're on the subject I hope we can be honest with each other – you seem like a very straight 'call a spade a spade' kind of a person and I like that. If I do anything to wind you up just let me know – I'm rubbish at mind reading. I'll even give up eggs – it's only 2 weeks after all. Assume the ban doesn't apply to the chocolate variety?

A few background facts, some of which you may already know. I grew up in the deepest, darkest West Midlands so I still get freakishly excited at seeing the sea. I am the youngest of 3 kids, and youngest by a long way too, so I'm used to being spoilt. I got the hiking bug from family holidays in North Wales when I was a kid. Heaven knows where I got the gin bug from as I was brought up strict Methodist – I can only assume there are a number of secrets still stashed in the family closet.

Fear not for I too am a bit of a lightweight these days. It always seems grossly unfair that when I was broke and in my 20s, I was bomb proof when it came to hangovers, whereas these days, when I can afford a decent bottle of gin, I get a hangover after a couple of drinks. This doesn't bode all that well for us does it, especially on the days when we'll be having tours and samples in the mornings before a long hike – is 'drunk in charge of a map' a thing?

You may also recall that I had a couple of large smacks on the head last year, the result of which is still a bit of a dent in my short-term memory. I turned up to stay with my brother last autumn for a few days while I was working and completely forgot to take any clothes with me (other than the ones I was wearing). Be prepared to remind me where my phone/glasses/cup of tea are, as I've a tendency to forget.

Still can't quite believe we're doing this – should be an ace adventure – and the weather had better behave too – though it has been unseasonably chilly of late.

Big love

Beth

22nd August, 09:27

It's CHILLY you say?! That means I'll find it positively arctic. Haven't worn a pair of trousers for months so you know what that's like trying to squeeze into them! May have to resort to stretchy leggings.

I have met a few people from social media in real life (for a quick coffee though, not an extended holiday for two). The interesting thing is that, so far, everyone has been exactly as I expected. No great surprises! It will be interesting to see how we find each other and – as you say – if we're honest with stuff, then no worries!

Funnily enough, people do describe me as fairly quiet. I might natter a bit and get wayyyy too over excited when we spot a gin sign looming up but am definitely not loud. I grew up in Manchester (the eldest child) and I think my love of gin might have been spurred by my dad giving me Babycham at Christmas (complete with cherry on stick) in one of those cute Bambi glasses. I must have been 13 or 14.

And PLEASE enjoy your eggy breakfasts! Nearly everyone chooses them for brekkie so I'm used to the exposure. No idea why I loathe them so much (texture and smell, I think). I remember scoffing boiled eggs and soldiers as a kid.

Karen

24th August, 10:56

Clearly I'm getting more philosophical as we near our launch day, but it strikes me that our letters so far have focused on what's bad about us and what we can't do – how terribly British! We've both tried putting each other off and it hasn't worked yet, so how about a letter focusing on our good points? I know it feels weird but let's give it a go!

I'm organised but pretty laid back and have an excellent sense of humour. Granted, sometimes I laugh at things I probably shouldn't, but I'd much rather have a laugh in this life than anything else. I avoid miserable TV like soaps and reality stuff (can't stand them!) and will instead watch anything funny – the IT Crowd and Big Bang Theory are current favourites, but I love curling up in bed and working my way through my boxed sets of Cheers and MASH (yes, I still have a DVD player!).

Creativity is my strong point, though I occasionally need to be reined in on practical grounds, and I am relentlessly optimistic and can generally see the good in most things and people. I also don't do game playing and don't enjoy spending time with people who do.

As we've mentioned I'm not fussy and will eat anything – honestly, stick me in front of any eatery and I'll find something to go with. I also have pretty low standards so won't fuss if any of our accommodation is less than sparkly. I once shared a hotel room in London with a mouse and didn't tell the management until the next day – I thought he was sweet (the mouse, not the manager) but I reported it as I feared the next guest may not be quite so willing to share.

So there you go – your challenge is to send me a letter with all your positive qualities or else this will just look like me going off on a big ego trip!

See you soon!

Bx

24th August, 13:45

Ooo my good points? Well let me think…

Well if I start off with something my son said this summer. He said that some of the things he liked about me were: my unfailing ability to be positive (though he did say it could get annoying sometimes: 'Mum, you've got to accept that occasionally, some things are just rubbish'). He also said I was very friendly, fun and saw the funny side of stuff.

One thing I never do (this is not a good point, just makes me different to most people) is watch TV. I got out of the habit years ago when I was madly busy and didn't have time for playing on the computer (stalking Facebook) and watching TV. So the TV time went. I'm not against it in any way, just never think to switch it on. So I never see movies either unless it's a rare family trip to the cinema. You can change me!

So… what else positive? It's hard to do this about yourself! I think I'm easy going. It's a humungous deal if I lose my temper – can't remember the last time but it would have been with my husband.

I am trusting. I believe that 99% of people are good, and mean well. So far, I haven't been badly let down on that. Obviously I've had bad things happen, but then no-one escapes that.

I think I've exhausted my good list! Now, if you want a longer list I can go back to the bad?

Kxx

30th August, 08:18

Yo Bazza

Your letter made me laugh – Steve says stuff like that to me! He says 'It'll be fine' will be written on my headstone. He's more of a pessimist and balances me out perfectly. I suppose I do have mild concerns that when two positive, 'let's go for it' people are left to their own devices trouble may be afoot – who will be there to rein us in?

He also tells me I'm like the character in Monty Python and the Holy Grail who hops around with both arms and a leg missing shouting that it's just a flesh wound. When I had my second fall last year, with blood coming out of my head (I subsequently needed 5 staples) and a broken hand that was rapidly inflating, instead of heading to the nearest hospital in Penrith, I demanded to be taken to Kendal as I needed to go to Asda afterwards. I'm just saying I need a grown-up around me sometimes.

Are you an owl or a lark? I'm more larkish and, these days, tend to keel over around 10:30 p.m. – that said I also get overly excited like a child and when that happens can struggle to switch my brain off and get to sleep. Many's the night Steve has switched out the light to get some sleep and I'm lying there complaining that I'm 'bored now'. In such situations a whisky nightcap usually does the trick – is that how it works with kids or is that frowned upon?

You may also need to slap me to stop me over-organising. The colour-coded itinerary sheets I keep sending through probably already tipped you off on that one. I really need to learn to 'go with the flow' a lot more – I have a freakish ability to know exactly what the time is even when I'm not wearing a watch. I also may look 'laid back' on the outside but please do not be fooled – inside I'll be making timetables and schedules. It looks a little like this:

Karen: Shall we stop for lunch now?

Beth: (smiling) Yes, why not, it looks like a perfect spot!

Beth's brain: allowing 35 mins for lunch then 30-minute miles after that we should make our final destination around 17:43.

Anyway, enough of the scare tactics – we meet in 3 days & the very first thing we'll be doing is drinking gin and having lunch, so I reckon we'll be just fine.

Big love

B

30th August, 09:39

Yes my husband Pete is my mega positivity dampener. I can really annoy him ...

Common example if we're deciding whether to do something:

Me: 'What's the worst that could happen?'

Him: 'Well we may lose our home and all our belongings.'

Me: 'We'll cope if that happens. Let's do it!'

I also drive him crazy by planning. I love planning. Just LOVE it. In fact I've enjoyed planning this trip so much that I probably won't even turn up now. My joy is complete. We have done trips almost around the world and I've planned for us to arrive at some hotel at, say, 13:32 p.m. (give or take 10 seconds), and yes, due to my obsession we bloody well have. Pete says it makes him feel like his whole life is planned out minutely until death.

I am definitely a lark these days. Used to love evenings but even 10:30 p.m. can be a stretch sometimes. You may have to slap my snoring form awake in the bar and manoeuvre me to bed. (Don't drink my gin.)

That's it for now – off to Millets down the road so I can grab some blister plasters and brag loudly that I'm now a real multi-day hiker.

Karen

What our friends had to say…

Not content with trying to scare each other off by letter we also opened the issue up to our Facebook friends. We both put up posts along the lines of 'You all know we're going on this mad adventure, so what does Beth/Karen need to know about me?' These are some of our favourite responses.

Beth's friends

Dear Karen. Think carefully before you challenge Beth, she quite honestly will be 'up for it'! – Pam Goulding

She's a rockstar at bandioke! – Jo Loake

All I know is that when you joined the family you made me look sane! – Philippa Pipe

You'll be fine Karen. Just make sure she takes her medication and give her gin regularly and I'm sure there will be no repeat of that unfortunate incident. – Paul Saunders

Beth is full of energy, warm, witty, funny, sweet and a teeny bit mad so you'll have a ball. If you have a wobble at any point during the two weeks, Beth will help put things into perspective and pull you through. She also does a fantastic rendition of 'Me & Mrs Jones' – Sharon Senior

Karen … we came over for dinner and we were served plop on a plate. Seriously – Caz Stewart

I worked with Beth for a few years, bloody best boss EVER ! Karen you will have a blast! – Helaine Brownhill

As long as you keep Mrs Pipe away from any sort of alphabet candles in M&S you'll be ok. Otherwise rude words will have to be made for all to see – Heather Murphy

Don't do it Karen! Everything you have heard is, probably, true and more! You will end up barmy as a box of frogs by the end! – Ian Mooney

You know Tigger from Winnie the Pooh … well imagine him at least 10 times more bouncy & maybe that's like our Beth … she is fabulous oh & the gin is compulsory along with anything marmite – Angelique Lund

Karen, Beth is great. Just don't let her feed wine to wild horses – Mark Warren

Ask her what she did with the bar towel when I introduced her to the local vicar! – Ruth Lewis

Karen's friends

Karen loves to walk and loves to eat, very cheery and lots of fun – I am sure you will have the best time – Susan Jackson

Totally into chocolate and wine. Loves to be out and about but equally happy at home chillin'. Enjoys the simple things in life xx – Carol Ackerley

Karen bakes mean brownies! – Kay Eracleous

Mum you always want to see the best in everyone, including yourself – you are always setting yourself new goals. You are extremely positive and very easy to get along with (if someone doesn't like you then there is definitely something wrong with them). You're a great motivator too Xx – Laura Clinton

A real 'yes' person (not just to wine, chocolate, food in general) and great company. Has been known to snort when laughing a lot – Joanna Ellis

Karen is VERY generous and will INSIST on buying expensive presents for her kayaking friends back in Cyprus – Christine Menzies

Though I don't know you very well Karen, I'd say you appreciate the good things in life... sun, great views, wonderful food and a glass of the red or white stuff! I also think that I follow Beth on Twitter. Have fun girls. Looking forward to hearing more X – Zoe Langley-Wathen

Karen you got what you asked for, ha ha ha, you are so much fun!! – Emmy Schipper

Mad as a March hare but lovely with it lol xx – Marion Doig Ne Clare

Karen is a great friend to be with always positive and wanting to enjoy life to the full! One crazy lady that will be a great companion that you can depend on. Needs regular feeding of chocolate and wine – Jennifer Clarke

Extremely dependable, great company and full of life, should be a good trip – Karen Hitchman

Just so as you know…

SOME OF THE PRODUCERS we met for this book are large enterprises who will welcome you with open arms if you want to go and see them. Others are tiny organisations of only 1 or 2 people brewing delicious gins, vodkas and other liqueurs in their back gardens, and are in no way geared up for visitors, so please don't track them down and bang on the door telling them that we sent you, or anything like that.

For absolute clarity these are the producers who *would* be delighted to see you (obviously people like Windermere Cruises and Cumbria Crystal would love to see you too and all their details are at the end of the book):

Stan Laurel Inn, Ulverston – stock pretty much everything that Shed 1 produces

Virginia House, Ulverston – restaurant, gin parlour and extensive range of local and national gins

Unsworth's Yard, Cartmel – visit the off licence, pop your head in their tiny brewery and enjoy your lunch in their courtyard

Burgundy's Bar, Kendal – home to Kendal Mint Cake Liqueur and a dozen or so lethal cocktails!

The Punch Bowl, Barrow's Green (near Kendal) – home to Kendal Mint Cake Vodka, other booze and almighty burgers; what more could you want?

Windermere Wines, Windermere – if you want a bottle of local booze, this is the place to go!

Dodd's, Ambleside – fabulous food and a full range of Lakes Distillery gins

Keswick Brewing Company, Keswick – drop in anytime but best to book ahead to hire a Twizy or take a brewery tour

The Lakes Distillery, Bassenthwaite – open year round with tours, tastings, shop and alpacas

The Rum Story, Whitehaven – open year round for informative tours and an excellent cafe and shop

A shed load of sun

By train	Ulverston station is on the Barrow-in-Furness line and the station is a short walk from the town centre
By bus	There are a number of local buses serving Ulverston, all of which stop a short walk from the town centre
By bike	Ulverston is served by Sustrans routes 70 and 700
By car	From the M6 follow the A580 towards Barrow-in-Furness. Stop when you get to Ulverston
On foot	N/A

DAY ONE: Ulverston

Beth

Rather fittingly the first steps of *Gin, Cake & Rucksacks* weren't taken across a windswept fell; they were taken along the streets of Ulverston towards the Stan Laurel Inn – a friendly and popular local pub named in honour of one of the town's most famous sons.

Ulverston is an interesting small town on the south coast of Cumbria overlooking Morecambe Bay. Refreshingly, it has managed to avoid being overrun by the usual national chain stores which turn so many other small towns into identikit versions of each other and is, instead, awash with small local businesses – you can still tell which shop used to be Woolworth's though (I find that in whichever town I'm visiting, even if I'm there for the very first time, you can always spot which store used to be Woolies – how on earth did they go under with branding that strong?)

If you're visiting for the first time it's worth allowing a day to explore as there are a myriad twisting back alleys to discover, many adorned with blue plaques filling you in on the local history. Some of the rows of shops, such as those along the bottom end of Market Street, have remained largely unchanged over the years, with only the passing cars reminding you that you're now in the twenty-first century.

Ulverston is very proud of its connections to Stan Laurel, who was born in the town on 16th June 1890. As well as the pub we were heading towards there's also the Laurel and Hardy Museum next to the cinema, although my favourite tribute has to be the florists in the centre of town who named themselves Floral and Hardy.

Most people arriving into Ulverston for the first time do so from the east and probably wonder why there's a lighthouse on top of a hill next to the town. Standing on Hoad Hill, known locally as The Hoad or simply Hoad, the lighthouse (or The Pepperpot as it is also known) is actually the Sir John Barrow Monument – a 30m replica of the Eddystone Lighthouse, though one of the conditions of its erection was that it should never have a light in the top. It was built in 1850 to commemorate Sir John Barrow, who was born in the town and went on to found the Royal Geographical Society. Ulverston is equally as fond of Sir John Barrow as they are of Stan Laurel, and there are plenty of information boards around The Hoad commemorating his life and many achievements. Sadly there are no florists named in his honour.

Having only met an hour or so previously, when I was very thankful to finally discover that Karen really was who she said she was and not a 20-stone biker named Barry from Milton Keynes, our conversation was still in the very polite stages. I'd run a poll on Twitter in the run up to our adventure asking, 'Would you go on a 2-week hike with someone you only knew through social media?' 40% said yes, 41% said no, and 19% said depends – though most of them didn't say what it depended on. If it depended on having plenty to drink then we were definitely going to be okay.

As we wound our way along the gloriously sunny back streets of Ulverston we chatted about our families, our hopes and fears for what the coming two weeks held, and what on earth we'd put in our rucksacks. Neither of us had done a multi-day hike before so neither of us really knew what to keep in and what to leave out. We were getting along just fine and we hadn't even started drinking yet; things were looking good.

When I'd laid all my stuff out on the bed at home my husband had commented on how modest it all looked, but it didn't feel very modest now it was all strapped to my back. I honestly thought I'd kept things to a bare minimum with just the essentials included; in the coming days I was going to redefine the meaning of the term 'essential' many times over.

My first impressions of Karen were that she seemed pretty much exactly the same as she did online, although irritatingly slimmer; I made a mental note not to exhale for the next two weeks. She seemed very organised and had packed and repacked her rucksack at our house before we set off. A shared purpose is said to be an excellent foundation for friendship, and as our shared purpose right now was a pub I figured our friendship would probably be just fine.

Beth (left) and Karen, at their first meeting

Our first meeting was with Andy and Zoe, the folks behind the curiously named Shed 1 Gin. One of our aims on this walk is to tell the individual stories of the producers we meet along the way. Before we set out we knew pretty much nothing about any of them and so had no idea what to expect; we could only hope that they'd have interesting stories to tell. We certainly weren't disappointed by Andy and Zoe, who set a pretty high bar for the others to clear.

Andy was (and still is) an actor and Zoe was (and still is) a teacher when they rather improbably first met in South Korea – one of those freakishly random sequences of events which would draw derision as a far-fetched plotline in a Hollywood rom-com but makes perfect sense in real life. Having travelled to the far-flung corners of the globe and conducted a ridiculously long-distance romance, they eventually decided to settle in Ulverston. On the day they moved into their house they were busy unpacking the removal van and directing people as to where to put the boxes. They had two sheds in the back garden and, for ease of direction, named them 'shed one' and 'shed two'. The names stuck and, having now built their still in 'shed one', this eventually led to the naming of the gin.

Our lessons in gin making were coming thick and fast. Shed 1 is not a London Dry Gin on account of the fact that to produce it distillers are required to adhere to a very strict set of European

directives, which are themselves drier than the driest Martini. In a nutshell, London Dry Gin must go through a very specific distillation process, be a minimum of 37.5% proof, contain no artificial ingredients and, crucially, cannot have any flavour added after distillation.

Shed 1 produce a classically distilled gin, but what makes them unique is the fact that they start by combining all their different flavours to produce a compound gin, which they then distil to fine tune it. Many other producers create the compound gin but don't distil it and this results in something which could technically be called a 'Bathtub Gin'— a name which had my mind drifting off to the possibilities of bathing in gin. The expression originated in the United States during the prohibition era when people concocted their illicit brews at home. As stills were hard to come by, and as a large receptacle for the alcohol was required, bathtubs seemed an obvious way to plug the gap. Obviously, because Shed 1 produce their gin commercially, bathtubs are not part of the production process (can you imagine the field day health and safety would have with that?), but I rather like the imagery.

These guys add some big, imaginative and all natural flavours before distilling in the classic London Dry Gin fashion, and they produce spirits around the 43% proof mark, with no flavours added after distillation has taken place – to be fair they don't need to as each of their gins has a unique and distinctive taste, and even adding tonic feels like a crime.

Shed 1 make a number of gins, all created from different combinations of botanicals and all very different in taste. Their testing process is typically thorough and involves inviting their neighbours around for a tasting party (you could probably identify where they live in Ulverston by looking for the previously unexplained spike in property prices). One of their gins – Giggle in the Ginnel – is named after a batch they brewed for a 50th birthday party, which proved so popular they added it to their regular repertoire. Not that the life of their neighbours is all about product testing; one of them helps out by storing Shed 1's bottles in their spare room.

As many of the botanicals as possible are sourced locally; they've even teamed up with a florist friend in Carnforth who will be helping grow and source ingredients in the future. They keep many of their production elements as close to home as possible too, with their label maker (graphic designer!) living just around the corner.

With the warm rosy glow of a few samples swishing around our insides we headed back out into the warm sunshine. At least I thought it was warm; Karen, more used to sunnier climes, asked if I knew of anywhere she could buy a hot water bottle. We decided to drop the rucksacks off at Virginia House, our accommodation for the night, because large rucksacks and small shops don't mix well. I'll admit it did feel a little odd being shown to our shared room when we'd only met a few hours earlier, but I was rather hoping the

The Hoad (or lighthouse that never was!) viewed from the Ulverston Canal

numerous large gins standing between us and bedtime would help to oil the wheels of friendship.

I would say we were lucky enough to nab the last remaining hot water bottle in Boots, but as it was beautifully sunny and everyone else was wondering around in light t-shirts, there wasn't exactly a lot of competition for it.

Our next stop was at Cumbria Crystal, makers of very fine glassware, who had kindly agreed to give us two beautiful lead crystal glasses so that we could enjoy all our gins in style on our journey. From their unassuming factory on the edge of town they produce crystal which graces the finest tables on earth. Their glasses have featured in James Bond films, Downton Abbey and Poldark, and their Helvellyn range is the crystal of choice in British embassies around the globe. Plus they make bespoke crystal for royalty worldwide, as well as unique collections for organisations such as Bentley.

During the week you can not only visit their shop, stocked to the rafters with fine crystal of every size and shape (a really good job we'd left our rucksacks behind!), but also watch the glass being blown on the premises. It takes 10–15 years to fully train their skilled blowers and engravers and 10–14 days to produce each glass. They are unashamedly top end and have meticulous attention to detail. If I were to tell you that all of the crystal they sell in their factory shop is a second you may have visions of chipped or shoddy glass, but not at all – in fact I'd defy you to find any fault with it whatsoever. Only a well-trained eye could point out a tiny air bubble or a variation in thickness between two apparently identical glasses.

The crystal-making process goes something like this: glass sand is melted down in a furnace; this is then blown, or moulded, into the basic shape required; the glass is put into another oven to cool for 24 hours, after which the glasses are marked up for carving; once carved the glasses are polished, which involves them being reheated to smooth and melt the edges, cooled for another 2 days and then dipped into a vat of polishing acid for precisely 38 minutes to bring out the shine. During this process they will pass through quality control 6 times and any glasses not making the grade end up back in the furnace and are recycled into something else.

After all that, they were trusting us to carry two glasses, in our

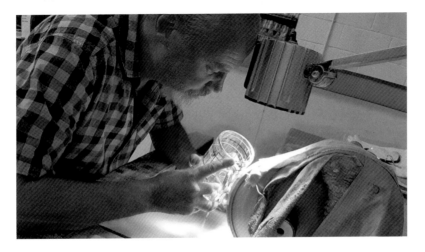

rucksacks, on a two-week drinking journey around the whole of Lakeland. You really have to admire their optimism.

The first journey the glasses took was just a mile or so to Canal Foot – the end point of Ulverston Canal, with stunning views down and across Morecambe Bay. It was such a beautifully sunny day that I wanted to show Karen some of the greener parts of town. Ulverston canal is only 2km long but is dead straight and flat and so made for the perfect walk for us to chat and get to know each other a little better. Pausing every now and again to admire an interesting bit of history (usually me) or an attractive flower (usually Karen) we spent our time filling in many of the gaps in our social media interaction – more family details, personal backgrounds and why so-and-so never replies to such-and-such posts – you know how it is on Facebook.

As the sun began to dip into Morecambe Bay we returned to Virginia House for dinner. Craig and Louise have been in charge there since 2015 and during that time they have gained an excellent reputation for fine dining, comfortable rooms and their extensive range of gins. When it's dry you can sit in the sun and enjoy a drink on the gin terrace behind the hotel, and when it's wet you can huddle up in their very well-stocked gin parlour.

The restaurant menu was imaginative, with everything cooked to perfection and beautifully presented, from the cold tomato soup and homemade bread at the start, to Westmorland cheese soufflé with parmesan custard that I chose to finish with (I don't have a sweet tooth and adore cheese in any guise). It was great to see the place so busy with everyone clearly having a very good time, and tables there are justifiably in high demand.

Stuffed to the gills we waddled into the gin parlour for a nightcap, where both of us opted for Bedrock Gin and realised that within the space of a few short hours we'd become 'gin snobs'. Whereas in the past it would have been enough to simply pour a gin, throw some decent tonic in it and pop in a slice of lemon or lime for good measure, now we needed to know more – what were the main botanicals in the gin, and therefore which tonics, mixers and/or garnishes would work best? Luckily Virginia House are way ahead of us on that one and their menu already makes the necessary recommendations. Because Bedrock Gin uses liquorice as one of its botanicals and therefore has a very slightly aniseed flavour, our G&T was served with a small bead of liquorice in the bottom of the glass and tasted absolutely perfect.

As the clock was now creeping towards midnight and as we had a long hike ahead of us the next day, we decided to call it a day and head for bed. It could have been the gin but by now it didn't feel like I was sharing a room with a stranger. We'd chatted so much during the day and already had so many laughs that it didn't feel too odd at all – mind you, I was still concerned that my snoring might keep Karen awake and I had to remember not to exhale and risk blowing a button off my trousers...

Karen

'You're not Barry!'

Beth's opening words as I wound down my car window symbolised the slightly ludicrous situation we'd set up for ourselves over the previous few weeks.

'Hi Beth.'

'Hi Karen.'

It started well; Beth had emerged from her house with a smile on her face and no visible weapons in hand.

Approaching Cumbria my nervousness had soared. Were we mad? What if we *really* didn't get on? What if my friends were right? It didn't help that the night before I'd read an article in *Backpacker* magazine which asked hikers: 'Would you resort to cannibalism if your life depended on it?' A shocking number of readers had said 'yes.'

Beth won't know this but I'd spent a frantic evening the week before our trip googling 'meeting a Facebook friend in person'. There's even an acronym for it. Meeting IRL (in real life).

Most advice suggested having something planned such as a meal, going shopping or a visit to a museum or gallery. No-one mentioned going away for two weeks together, and all vehemently discouraged sleeping together on the first night.

I did actually know of one friend who had met a few of her Facebook acquaintances for coffee and she dismissed my fears.

'It'll feel surprisingly normal,' she insisted. 'If you've already chatted a lot online then you're not strangers. Chances are they'll be similar in person.'

'So no great surprises?' I asked.

'The only shock I regularly have is how much taller or shorter they are than I was expecting.'

I was pretty much a newbie to Cumbria too, having only visited twice before. I was excited to be returning yet not quite sure what to expect. I knew that many people had a huge love affair going with the place and that it was home to six times more sheep than people.

I'd also had a quick google about our first port of call, Ulverston.

I clicked on a site which promised me 'interesting and historical facts about Ulverston', only to read 'Sorry, there are no interesting facts about Ulverston.'

I dug deeper and found that Ulverston's famous son Stan Laurel and I shared the same birthday. Not the year, I hasten to add. Since he was regularly described as 'the tall, thin, dumb one' I was hoping that the similarity ended there.

When I'd finally tucked my car into its spot for the next two weeks I lugged my rucksack into Beth and Steve's house and logged on to their wifi. My phone pinged incessantly with incoming messages from fretting friends and family.

'Are you there yet? Sniff any drink you're offered!'

'Have you worked out what cult it is yet?'

And from an ex-flying friend, 'Check your nearest exit!'

I needn't have worried. Within minutes we were chatting over coffee and sharing our reservations about what lay ahead, both hoping that the other would turn out to be less speedy, less of a mountain goat and slower to spot a glass of gin coming our way.

And my friend had been right. During that first meeting Beth was just as I'd imagined; friendly, chatty and engagingly optimistic. One of her rucksack essential items was one of those jumbo multicolour ballpoint pens and I recently sent her a wildly colourful image with the text: 'Life is about using the whole box of crayons'. She's like that.

It was nearly time to get ready. But first, a little surprise. Cumbrian musician and storyteller Steve Wharton had recorded a song and dedicated it to Beth and I to wish us good luck on our 'spirit trail' across Cumbria. What a lovely gesture!

Standing on the floor on its flimsy base, my rucksack was almost as long as my legs. I'd always loved hiking but had never done a multi-day hike before, and never carried more than some fudge, a fleece and a flask. A tight knot of apprehension sat in my stomach as I fretted over carrying the inevitable weight.

Beth and I had the same rucksack, which we'd been sent to trial after successfully bidding to blog for the outdoor company Berghaus a few years back. Whatever I did and however hard I tried, for the first couple of days of the trip, Beth's rucksack always looked neater and more compact than mine. I gave up in the end, simply vowing to sort it out at some stage.

I repacked the rucksack for the third time. It was still too heavy. What could I take out? I considered leaving my Hydroflask behind. The company had kindly sent us one each to accompany our trip but with weight in mind every item counted. As I held the empty flask in my hand, I considered leaving it behind. In the end I slid it into the side pocket and, as the days progressed, was extremely glad that I had.

Eventually I decided on:

2 x leggings
2 x tops
2 x walking shirts
2 x walking trousers
1 x pair socks (plus wearing one)
Nightshirt
No room for shoes – flip flops would have to do
6 x knickers
Dress (ever optimistic)
Kindle/pad/pen
Hydroflask
Toiletries
Waterproof jacket and pants
Hairstyler and gas (totally unnecessary treat)
Jelly babies and mini malt loaves
Glasses and sunglasses
Money
Medication
Phone
Charger
Phone case and credit cards
Camera and mini tripod

Beth's husband Steve gave us a lift to Ulverston, where we tumbled out of the car and hefted our rucksacks onto our backs.

We were off.

If you'd asked me before if I knew much about gin I'd have been quietly confident enough to say that I did. Today, however, my gin education was just about to begin.

Before the day was out I'd done the impossible: managed to find room in my rucksack for more absolute essentials. In went the most beautiful and heavily bubble-wrapped lead crystal glass, courtesy of Cumbria Crystal, plus two small bottles of Shed 1 Gin and – joy of joys – a hot water bottle. Beth was positively basking and peeling off

It's the Ulverston Beer Festival Oli. Let's Go!

This is another fine mess you've got me into!

layers in the Cumbrian sunshine, but having spent the previous six months in Cyprus I was struggling to maintain body temperature.

We turned the corner into Queen Street and there was our room for the night: Virginia House, an elegant Georgian town house with a handful of steps to take us to the entrance. I instantly loved the décor. Since they took over in 2015, owners Craig and Louise Sherrington have been gradually restoring the place, and they've used a lot of the grey that is super popular at the moment. Pewter, steel, stone, slate. It looks terrific; stylish and smart.

As Craig went off to sort out our keys, we couldn't resist poking our heads into the room for which we'd carried high hopes for days now: the hotel's very own gin parlour.

'Later,' we agreed. 'Too soon to get excited. Better go for a walk or something.'

Peering through a window, as we went up to our room, I spotted just the place for a wind-down G&T – a pretty walled garden with comfy chairs, cushions and fluffy blankets.

If our room was anything to go by, the furnishings and facilities are of a high standard here; there is everything you need. I tucked my little hot water bottle under the pillow before Beth could find it and bin it.

We couldn't resist a stroll in the early evening sun and ended up following the short stretch of canal towpath which heads out to the coast at Morecambe Bay. It's only just over a mile long and claims to be UK's shortest, widest and deepest.

We must have been subconsciously saving ourselves for the days to come, as even the ducks were moving faster than we were. I had a good feeling about our trip and knew that we'd make it work.

Reaching the coast we stood awhile enjoying the views towards the Leven viaduct and over Morecambe Bay, before retracing our steps, spurred on by the prospect of supper at Virginia House.

Google had told me that Craig was Michelin-trained and had been causing quite a stir on the local gastronomic scene. From all I'd experienced here so far, I had high expectations for the food to come. We settled into our seats in the smart black, grey and cream dining room, the tables having just the right spacing between them; one bugbear of mine is being squeezed in and overhearing every word uttered by my neighbouring diners.

We dithered over whether to order the veritable feast of the multi-course Cumbrian tasting menu, but plumped instead for a starter, main and dessert, each accompanied by the recommended wine. Louise served us with an *amuse-bouche* of chilled tomato water and – I ask you – whenever have two hikers been able to resist the bread basket? Nigh on impossible if it's served like this: hot mini loaves with generous curls of creamy butter. I'd ordered fish so felt confident I had left the necessary bread space.

It was one of those meals where the presentation is so exquisite that you steel yourself before plunging a knife in. More importantly, every single thing tasted as good as it looked. Craig is most definitely a chef to watch out for.

By the time we were offered the dessert menu we were so full and sated that we'd given up talking. I was trying to mentally work out whether we could build our entire

Flavouring the gin –
top secret recipe

walk from here, padding back to base after we'd tucked away the daily mileage.

'Definitely no dessert,' groaned Beth.

Then she spotted an intriguing concoction on the dessert menu: a soufflé of smoked Westmorland cheese, parmesan custard and tomato jam. The cheese fanatic in her won out.

I was getting worried. 'Save a space for the gin, girl!'

As the gin parlour was very dark it added to the impression that something rather thrilling and delicious awaited us and we managed to sidle in almost unnoticed. The only real illumination came from the bar area where a broadly smiling young lass was already selecting two of those fabulous, oversized goblets that the gin world has so embraced in recent years.

It all started with Spanish chefs who were none too pleased – ¡Ay no! – to find that the ice cubes in their drinks were melting far too quickly in the steamy kitchens. Some bright spark discovered that ice cubes survived longer in a balloon-type glass. A glass this shape also allows you to poke your nose in a little further so you get a full blast of the aromas. As your sense of smell heavily influences your perception of taste (and with all the experimentation with adding botanicals to gins nowadays) it's easy to see why this is a great glass for a gin and tonic.

I'm so glad the young girl in Virginia House's gin parlour took us in hand. She turned out to be extremely knowledgeable and I would have struggled to choose. So many gins – more than 60! The staff here are fabulous and will suggest gins to try, plus mixers and garnishes, if you – like me – are a little stumped.

We settled down, nursing a balloon of Bedrock Gin, with a little bead of liquorice bobbing around in the tonic bubbles. Divine.

We dragged our tired selves up to bed and were soon fast asleep. Beth had repeatedly apologised in advance for her tendency to snore so of course it was me who loudly snorted myself awake in the middle of our very first night.

Spirit/liqueur info sheet

Product	Shed 1 Gin The three standard gins are: Cuckold's Revenge (Great Taste Award), Giggle in the Ginnel and Fancy Frolic. Limited edition seasonal gins: for Christmas, Festive Tipple, and for, Valentine's Day, Shed Loads of Love.
Category	Craft Gin Cuckold's Revenge 44% ABV Giggle in the Ginnel 43% ABV Fancy Frolic 43% ABV Festive Tipple 43% ABV Shed Loads of Love 41% ABV
Who makes it?	Andy and Zoe Arnold-Bennett
When did it start production?	October 2016
Where is it made?	In a shed in Ulverston...
Key ingredients	**Cuckold's Revenge** Classic base of juniper and coriander balanced with cardamom and star anise, rounded with fresh orange and lemon zest with a hint of cinnamon. **Giggle in the Ginnel** Star anise and angelica join with elderberry and fresh orange zest. **Fancy Frolic** A delicate blend of lime leaf, flower and fresh zest, a hint of ginger and strawberry. **Festive Tipple** Christmas in a glass! A smooth mix of festive flavours including cinnamon, nutmeg, cloves, sultanas and cherries with lightly sweetened orange and lemon zest. **Shed Loads of Love** A sumptuous celebration of love! Rose petals, lavender and strawberries with a delicate hint of chilli to bring a little heat to the proceedings.
Where can I buy it?	Visit the website for an ever increasing list of stockists https://www.shed1distillery.com/stockists Online shop https://www.shed1distillery.com/shop
Best way to drink it?	'The first time you try it, I always just recommend drinking it straight or with a clean tonic. After that, you can add any garnish you think suits it,' said Andy.

A couple of soaked old soaks

By train	Cark and Cartmel station is on the Barrow-in-Furness line and is 1.7 miles from the village of Cartmel
By bus	There are a number of local buses serving Cartmel throughout the year – search South Lakeland buses for up to date timetables
By bike	Cartmel is served by Sustrans routes 70 and 700
By car	From Ulverston follow the A590 to Backbarrow then follow the signs along local roads to the village centre. Parking is adjacent to the racecourse. NB if driving do be aware that on race weekends the village is very busy and parking is very hard to find
On foot	Our route took us from Ulverston, behind Hoad Hill and down into Greenodd. From there we crossed the footbridge and followed the public footpath to Low Wood, then climbed Bigland Hill and passed Bigland Tarn. When we reached the road at Grassgarth we continued along the road and dropping down into Cartmel

Distance = 10 miles

DAY TWO: Ulverston to Cartmel

Beth

We soaked up the last of the previous night's gin with a superb breakfast of epic proportions. Craig and Louise then left their other guests to fend for themselves for a few minutes and, with their daughter in tow, came to see us off as we began our adventure proper. With everyone waving and people peering out of windows to see what was going on, we were off! We turned the corner of the first street and I consulted the map.

'We're going the wrong way,' I muttered to Karen.

'What?'

'We're going the wrong way,' I said a little louder.

'Oh.'

'Is anyone still looking?'

'No idea.'

'Let's just keep going and we'll double back further on,' I suggested. This wasn't quite the glorious departure I'd had in mind. I wondered if this had ever happened to my hero Commander Scott when he set out for the South Pole. Had he ever confidently set out from the hut at Cape Evans only to realise he was going the wrong way and had to loop round a large rocky outcrop and hope no-one had noticed? Unlikely.

Having been gloriously sunny the previous day, and indeed all through breakfast, the rain now arrived. Gently at first, but still rain. We navigated the back streets of Ulverston before making our way up onto Hoad Hill, where the wind, and the rain, soon picked up. This was so annoying! I'd really wanted to show Karen the very best views in Cumbria (and pretend that it never rains) and here we were, passing one of my favourite spots and all I could lamely say was 'the views are usually beautiful from here,' as I snapped a photo of the Hoad monument against a backdrop of thick grey clouds.

I have a real thing for history, and my first clue that Karen didn't quite share this love was when I stood reading the information board for the Hoad in the pouring rain with a big grin on my face. I know the history of the Hoad, but I still love looking at the old schematics and

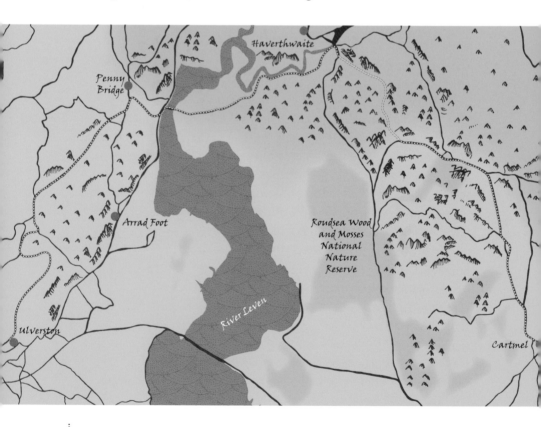

Bigland Woods, very Lord of the Rings

pondering how they did it all without the aid of computers. Karen seized the opportunity to layer up the waterproofs. Wise move.

There was no getting away from the fact that the weather was foul, so we pushed on, over the top of the hill and down into the shelter of the valley beyond, tucking into the plentiful blackberries along the way. The track we followed around to Newlands Bottom Farm was clearly an ancient route – you know, one of those deep paths with overgrown tops that you can imagine people travelling along hundreds of years ago. Or at least I could. Karen was beginning to get the measure of my weirdness but, to be fair, she was still being very polite about it. Well, either that or she still had a mouthful of blackberries.

The rain continued the entire way into Greenodd, where we paused for a breather. I was trying to impress Karen with how hardy and self-sufficient we Cumbrians are when we passed a headline board for the local newspaper outside a nearby shop. 'Ulverston man's frog in the bog dilemma' it screamed. I had trouble explaining that one. (For the record it was a story about a local man who called the RSPCA to rescue a frog from his toilet – not really showing us in our best light.)

From Greenodd the plan was to head across the estuary and aim for Bigland Tarn before continuing on to Cartmel. By now the wind had dropped and the rain had mostly stopped, but not completely. This meant that we kept our waterproofs on, even though it was now jolly warm, resulting in us perspiring so much that we ended up soaked to the skin and would have been better off without them anyway.

'Any hills today?' asked Karen.

'Erm,' I replied, peering through the murky greyness towards Bigland Hill, 'not by Lake District standards.'

Karen followed my gaze. 'Oh.'

To be fair, the last time I'd been up Bigland Hill I'd been on a bike completing the Morecambe Bay Cycleway. Well, I say 'on a bike', more like 'beside a bike', as I'd given up after the first 100 yards or so and pushed it up. But today we weren't on the road, we were on the forest track, and I'd traded the bike for a huge rucksack, which probably weighed about the same but sadly didn't have wheels.

The weather conditions meant that the track up through Bigland Woods had a distinctly Middle Earth air about it and we arrived at Bigland Tarn just in time to see it before the mist rolled down and obscured it completely. I could tell you it looked mysterious and ethereal, which is just another way of saying it was foggy and we couldn't see much – apart from one half-dead tree near the edge of the tarn, perfectly positioned for the taking of moody Ansell Adams-style photographs.

Due to the inclement weather conditions and rather soupy nature of the ground underfoot, we abandoned our cross-country route and instead took the road down into Cartmel, where along the way there was a really odd coincidence. As we descended the hill towards the village Karen peered over a nearby drystone wall and pointed out some pretty cottages.

'Oh, they're Crumble Cottages,' I said, 'a couple of beautiful holiday cottages, and they belong to some of friends of ours.'

A hundred yards or so further on we passed a road junction, and who should arrive at exactly the same time but the owners of the cottages, Sarah and Stewart, just on their way to the shops. That's exactly the sort of coincidence I wouldn't believe if I read it in a book but I swear that's precisely how it happened. We didn't fight them off too hard when they insisted on dragging us back to their place for tea and biscuits. As Sarah gave Karen the guided tour (they

lovingly renovated the cottages and gardens themselves and they are absolutely stunning) me and Stewart put the world to rights over our shared love of connecting people with the history right on their doorstep – neither of us had particularly enjoyed history lessons at school, but now we couldn't get enough of it and were sharing new and exciting ways of inflicting our enthusiasm onto others. Far too soon it was time to be on our way again.

As we made our way into the village we passed Cartmel Racecourse, where I showered poor Karen with a whole plethora of 'did you knows' about its history – things like the fact that races have been run there since the early 1800s, that it has the longest run in (distance from the final fence to the finish line) of any racecourse in the country, and that all the winners are given a Cartmel Sticky Toffee Pudding to take home with them. Her ears pricked up at that last nugget and I practically had to drag her past the Sticky Toffee

Pudding shop in the centre of the village. I was busy pointing out the fishstones that mark the sight of an ancient market, but I'm not sure I had her full attention.

In the middle of the village, very near to the fishstones in fact, is the Royal Oak, purveyors of superb beers and makers of the finest tomato soup on the planet. It was here that we had arranged to meet Judith, the woman behind Kin Toffee Vodka.

Judith is a force to be reckoned with and had walked away from a career in financial services after deciding that there must be more to life. She worked at nearby Holker Hall for a while as a retail manager and began making toffee vodka in her spare time as gifts for family and friends. She'd been inspired by tasting something similar in France and decided to have a go at making it herself.

By now she'd moved on to work at Brathay Hall and, being the lovely person that she is, took a few bottles in to give away in a fundraising event. From there she got more and more requests for it, until she decided to 'go for it', sort all the legal stuff out and sell it properly.

To begin with the entire operation ran from her kitchen, the labels were designed locally, and she started off going from door-to-door with bottles in her bag, persuading people to sample and stock the drink. From there she progressed to food festivals. In September 2014 she properly founded the company, and over Christmas 2016 her product was stocked by John Lewis. She now supplies Booths, where she was named Supplier of the Year for 2016 and, while we're on the subject of awards, she also won the Cumbria Life Producer of the Year in 2016 – all of which proves her hunch was right; there really is more to life than financial services.

She lives in Newby Bridge and during Storm Desmond in December 2015 she was flooded out, but still did not miss one single order. 'We were sloshing around in our wellies,' she said, 'but we got them all out.' As I said, she's a force to be reckoned with.

The drink is a beautiful, rich, deep golden-brown colour and, although I'd shied away from flavoured vodkas in the past thinking they might be too sickly, this one really isn't at all. It's rich and warm and was utterly perfect after a long soggy walk. It's also apparently great to cook with, as it doesn't split cream and it makes an excellent addition to puddings and cocktails. There are a number of recipes

The bridge at Low Wood,
Grade II listed

on Judith's website (see list of websites etc. on page 186), but it's definitely worth experimenting and discovering some of your own.

As we swayed out into the early evening (I'd like to say sunset here, but it was still overcast) I was quite thankful that we only had to make it as far as the hotel. It's an uphill route which I've walked many times as it's not too far from home but, for some strange reason, I didn't really notice the hill this time. Most odd.

However much I wanted to collapse into a hot bath as soon as I got into my room, the reality was that if I wanted some clean clothes in the morning I was going to have to wash them first. One of the 'luxuries' in my rucksack was a small plastic tub of Daz (the other was a travel-sized bottle of hair conditioner) and I quickly got to work washing, then drying as best I could by wringing things out in a towel and lining the now blazing-hot radiators around the room. Pretty soon the atmosphere became sauna-like and, as I finally sank into a deep, hot bubble bath, I made a mental note to tell Judith of another great use for toffee vodka – it tastes fabulous in hot chocolate.

Karen

It started raining the minute we waved our goodbyes to the folks at Virginia House. There was slight confusion as we descended the hotel steps then both turned ready to head off in different directions. Was it really going to be possible not to get lost over the next fourteen days?

As we headed for the hills the rain fell steadily, so we stopped amongst the sodden sheep to pull on our backpack waterproof covers. This was no mean feat as they flapped around like parachutes in the wind. My feet were wet already; I'd obviously skimped on the boot waterproofing. We squeezed ourselves and our packs through and over stiles and trudged on. Now, swathed head to toe in GORE-TEX, I couldn't even reach my jelly babies. Someone was looking out for me, though, as the bushes lining our route were studded with enormous blackberries.

I was feeling mildly anxious, knowing that many miles lay ahead of us, and I could already feel my backpack dragging; I still hadn't fitted it correctly, it seemed. Ahead of me, Beth appeared to be far more comfortable with her pack and it sat neatly on her hips.

A friction burn was already niggling at the base of my spine.

I thought back to secondary school when we would never have dreamed of using both straps on a backpack. We'd shove in a dozen library books and then hoist the pack onto one shoulder only; two was decidedly uncool. Well, the grown-up me craved comfort, not cool. That night, I vowed to fix this pack once and for all.

As a temporary fix I smeared a bit of chafing balm onto my back and ensured that my clothes were lying smooth underneath; as I've learned as I've got older, a few wrinkles anywhere can make a big difference.

'I'm not going out in that! Wait, did you say coffee and walnut?'

We were bathed in green as we climbed up Bigland Hill on a narrow, rocky path through dripping, overhanging trees, the sound of rushing water everywhere. It was incredibly soothing, like playing my rainforest sounds CD, back in the car. After having spent the previous several months in dry, baked Cyprus I stopped frequently to deeply inhale the fresh, earthy aromas. And then Bigland Tarn was before us, silent and moody in the heavy mist which hung over the water, a lone tree piercing its surface.

Hauling off the backpacks we stopped by the tarn to refuel on jelly babies and coffee, which was still steaming hot thanks to our Hydroflasks. They proved to be an absolute boon throughout our trip as they kept our drinks hot for over six hours.

As we carried on, and prompted by the blackberries, I was rambling in a different way – about the simple joy of finding nature's bounty of tidbits to snack on as you go.

'I just love eating things I find on the way!' I enthused.

A lone sheep gave me a look of horror before bolting up the hill.

Juicy morsels on the hedgerows were thin on the ground for the next hour, though, so we dumped our rucksacks with a thud by a wall and tucked into a Higginson's Huntsman pie before tackling the last mile or so into Cartmel.

As we reached the outskirts of the village, we passed by the idyllically situated and named Crumble Cottages, and by chance bumped into the owners, Sarah and Stewart, who kindly invited our soggy selves in for tea and biscuits.

This engaging and enthusiastic couple have renovated a lovely 500-year-old Cumbrian longhouse and converted the attached barn into luxury holiday lets. Think soft, soothing colours, fluffy towels, oak beams, thick walls and chandeliers.

When I tell you that Sarah is a horticulturalist and garden designer, you may start to get an inkling of the stunning gardens surrounding the property. There's a wildflower meadow, orchards, a water garden and a fruit and vegetable kitchen garden with the biggest raspberries I'd ever seen!

Did we really have to leave? It wasn't only me, though; the local wildlife has homed in too and loves to linger at Crumble Cottages.

The first thing I saw as we approached Cartmel was the Village Shop, the home of Cartmel Sticky Toffee Pudding. From tiny beginnings, when Jean Johns first began stirring up her sinfully rich mix to boost takings in what was then the post office, production of their luscious puddings now tops a million a year, exporting far and wide.

I pressed my nose mournfully against the shop window; Cartmel was my first experience of 'you can't go in shops with a rucksack this

No brainer!

size on your back'. Don't tell my husband; he'd have one permanently fused to my spine.

For such a tiny, unassuming place, Cartmel boasts an astonishing number of gourmet treats. It's a food and wine lover's paradise. Even more jaw dropping is that in 2014 the *New York Times* put Cartmel on its worldwide 'must visit' list, placing it ahead of Vienna, Nepal and Niagara Falls!

So what's all the fuss about?

First, there's the beauty. There's a 12th-century priory, a Victorian racecourse and an assortment of 16th–18th-century buildings clustered around the village square.

Then there's those mysterious magic hands; whenever the local folk turn their hands to food and drink they invariably strike gold.

Aside from the huge success of the Sticky Toffee Pudding, Cartmel Coffee has been rated one of the top ten cafes in the country. There's also an award-winning cheese shop and a microbrewery, and I nearly walked right past the unassuming little entrance to L'Enclume.

Run by chef Simon Rogan, L'Enclume has received high praise indeed. The *Good Food Guide* named L'Enclume as the top UK restaurant for four years running. How I wished we were staying to sample the 20-course tasting menu.

But it was time to hear about a winning blend of toffee and vodka. We were meeting Judith Wren of Kin Toffee Vodka and were keen to hear her story.

It all started with a little après ski tipple in France. The toffee vodka was so warming, smooth and delicious that Judith knew she couldn't just fly home and forget about it.

A self-confessed dabbler, Judith 'messed about for a few years' trying to come up with her own version of toffee vodka. With family and friends as testers, she kept going until she got the thumbs up.

'I knew it was good,' Judith told us, 'so I started bottling it with a jug and funnel in my kitchen. I then stuck some labels on. To be honest, my aim was to see if I could sell a few bottles and pay for a ski pass!'

Judith started taking her vodka to local markets and food festivals with her husband, Mike, who had stepped in as chief bottler. The vodka proved so popular that they just rolled their sleeves up in their Newby Bridge kitchen and kept going.

The next stage was to get a natty design created for the brand, and find a bottler.

'The idea behind the name is "kith and kin", as it's something to be shared with the people who you care for,' said Judith.

The label is a dark grey colour to suggest Lakeland slate, and the view depicted is of the Langdale Pikes from Gummer's How. The little wren is a reference to Judith's surname.

'It's me in a bottle,' says Judith.

With such a local feel to her branding you'd be right in thinking that Judith is a proud Cumbrian. She has lived and worked in the area all her life, going to school in Ulverston and later working for the Furness Building Society, and as a business manager at Brathay Trust in Ambleside. Nowadays, she focuses solely on producing her Kin Toffee Vodka.

Judith still makes her vodka at her home in an old blacksmiths in Newby Bridge. She doesn't distil the vodka herself; the secret is in her unique toffee recipe which is blended with the spirit.

It's down to Judith's determination and belief in her product – 'I just stuck some bottles in a bag and went off around the shops' – that Kin Toffee Vodka has grown much faster than she expected. In 2016, she was awarded Supplier of the Year by Booths, and *Cumbria Life* Producer of the Year. Kin Toffee Vodka is now stocked in hundreds of locations across the UK.

And if you hanker after doing something similar yourself, Judith has a message for you: 'Don't worry about what anyone else is doing, you can't change that. Just do the best you can.'

Kin Toffee Vodka is sold in the Cartmel Village Shop along with a sticky toffee pudding in the 'Pudding and Kin' gift pack. Surely a match made in heaven.

We slogged up the hill to Uplands Hotel, our bed for the night. After some essential rinsing of smalls and placing of my soggy boots on the radiator, I focused on readjusting my pesky backpack. Tipping everything out, I logged onto the wifi and decided to start from scratch; by following the backpack's instructions.

After parading in front of a mirror I realised that the pack was too long for me so the first thing I did was adjust the torso length. That was better; the hip belt was now, pleasingly, in the hip region. I knew that, when correctly fitted, the hip belt would transfer lots of the weight off my shoulders and onto my hips. I could then use my legs, the biggest muscles in my body, to carry most of the weight.

I wasn't feeling too embarrassed by my obvious ignorance of backpacking basics; I've been surprised over the years to see many instances of poorly fitted packs like mine, with plenty of hikers sporting hip belts dangling around their legs, their shoulders sagging with the weight.

After repacking the rucksack I hoisted it back on and spent the next 10 minutes adjusting straps and buckles; now I was happy to face the next day.

Spirit/liqueur info sheet

Product	Kin Toffee Vodka
Category	Spirit drink 20.3% ABV
Who makes it?	Judith Wren
When did it start production?	September 2014
Where is it made?	Newby Bridge
Key ingredients	Toffee and caramel with vodka
Where can I buy it?	Independent retailers, Booths, Moonpig and many more https://kinvodka.co.uk/pages/stockists

Best way to drink it?

Best enjoyed chilled over ice. With virtually anything but tonic!

For more cocktail recipe ideas visit https://kinvodka.co.uk/pages/mixology

Some ideas...

TOFFEE APPLE
50ml Kin Toffee Vodka
50ml apple juice
25ml lemon juice
Serve with an apple slice

TOFFEE LEMON BON BON
25ml Kin Toffee Vodka
25ml Limoncello
200ml low sugar lemonade
Ice and a slice in a glass.

BANOFFEE
50ml Kin Toffee Vodka
50ml banana liqueur
10ml single cream
1/4 banana
Blend together

CINNAMON TOFFEE
50ml Kin Toffee Vodka
50ml cinnamon Schnapps
50ml apple Juice

SOUR KIN
50ml Kin Toffee Vodka
25ml lemon juice
25ml sugar syrup
Ice – shake it all about!

GINGER KIN WARMER
50ml Kin Toffee Vodka
50ml cloudy apple juice & ginger

QUICK KIN ESPRESSO
Plan ahead...
Freeze espresso coffee into ice cube trays. Take a glass, add two ice cubes, pour a good measure of Kin on top. Sit down. Relax.

MILK KIN SHAKE
300ml chilled full fat milk
150ml Kin Toffee Vodka
Pinch of cinnamon
Scoop of ice cream (optional)
Whizz together, pour and add a straw!

JACK-KIN
50ml Jack Daniels bourbon
75ml Kin Toffee Vodka

KIN KIR ROYALE
Champagne, cava or prosecco
Slug of Kin Toffee Vodka

Tinker, tailor, soldier, cry...

By train	No stations nearby
By bus	No buses
By bike	No Sustrans routes pass through Bowland Bridge, however the walking route was along quiet country lanes ideal for cycling
By car	From Newby Bridge follow the A592 towards Bowness then turn right to follow the local road opposite Fell Foot Park. This will take you steeply uphill past Gummer's How and on into Bowland Bridge. Turn right here to reach Cowmire
On foot	We followed the road from Cartmel to High Newton. From there we followed Height Road all the way to Goswick Hall then right to Bowland Bridge and right again to Cowmire

Distance = 8 miles

DAY THREE:
Cartmel to Cowmire

Beth

Ever had one of those times when you have a brilliant idea about 12 hours too late? Well that's exactly what happened to me, and is the best excuse I have for why we had a gin and tonic with our breakfast.

The previous evening, in the Uplands Hotel, we'd enjoyed a fine dinner, where we added wine to our already extensive list of drinks for the day. The place was pretty quiet and the owner was chatting to us about where we were from and what we were doing. Once he knew we were on a gin quest he was keen to show us the many fabulous gins in his collection, one of which changed colour when tonic water was added to it. Now, don't ask me why, but it didn't occur to me at that moment that we should sample the gin, film it changing colour, and post on our social media streams.

As I blearily clawed my way into consciousness on the morning of day three the idea finally landed with a bump. 'We really should have ordered that and filmed it,' I thought, rather too quickly followed by,

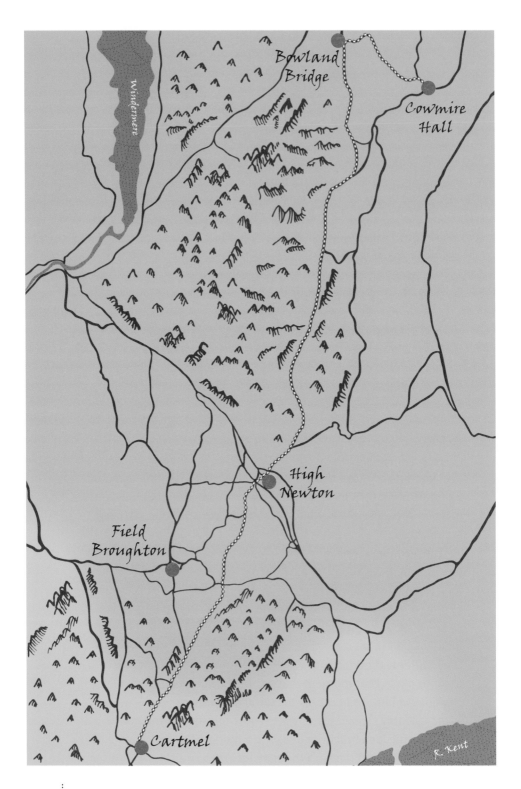

'I wonder if we can do it this morning with breakfast?' This trip was getting me into some very bad habits.

Talking of bad drinking habits, in an effort to improve my general wellbeing and understand exactly how much of a lie my 'yeah, I drink around 14 units a week, honest' statement was every time I completed a medical questionnaire, I had downloaded the Drinkaware app to my phone and logged every single drink I'd had over the course of the previous year. I stopped recording a couple of weeks prior to this trip, which is perhaps as well because even at this early stage the app would probably have been accessing my contacts list and sending urgent texts to my family and friends recommending an intervention at the earliest available opportunity.

The other downside to the app was that it offered you, at the tap of a button, the opportunity to register weak spots – places where you were prone through habit (or family) to indulge in a drink. Now, like many people, I enjoy a drink at home after a long day at work so I'd tagged home as one of my 'weak spots,' meaning that whenever I approached home a friendly little message would pop up, reminding me that I was near said 'weak spot' and offer me some wise words of encouragement.

Unfortunately, for me, it had the opposite effect and on many occasions I'd return home after a perfectly lovely day out and be looking forward to a nice cup of tea when my phone would buzz with my 'weak spot' alert causing me to stop and think to myself, 'what an excellent idea, yes I think I will have a G&T after all'! I wonder if I should feed that back to them?

Anyway, back to gin for breakfast. The Sharish Blue Magic Gin isn't made in Cumbria but it does change colour from deep blue to pink when mixed with tonic. Karen didn't seem quite as warmly enthusiastic as I'd expected when it came to knocking back a gin with her cornflakes, but then she didn't require that much persuading either. When I was a kid, back in the days when bringing up kids was rather less about creating a sterile bubble and rather more about just letting them get on with it, it wasn't considered to be a proper Boxing Day unless we'd had sherry trifle for breakfast. And I mean proper homemade sherry trifle that was heavy on the sherry and light on the trifle, so to me, gin for breakfast was the next logical step.

It definitely created a stir in the dining room as we filmed the gin changing colour – to be fair it wasn't all that dramatic but it was a nice little gimmick and an excellent way to start the day, especially as the rain was steaming down outside.

As we sloshed our way down into Cartmel my mind took off on one of its flights of fancy – I'd like to tell you that this was the result of the alcoholic breakfast, but as my husband Steve will verify, I don't require alcohol to head off to la la land.

'What if houses could fly?' I pondered aloud.

Karen looked at me a little oddly. 'What?'

'I said, what if houses could fly? Wouldn't that be cool? You could just take off and live wherever you wanted to.'

'Is this what happens when you have gin for breakfast?'

'No, this is the usual sort of random madness I talk about on long walks. It passes the time.'

The look on Karen's face suggested I should perhaps stick to less bizarre topics of conversation if I wanted to make it to Whitehaven in one piece. Luckily, at that precise moment she was saved by someone bursting out of a nearby house and asking if we were the two ladies doing the gin book. That happened a few times and it was rather lovely to think there were people actually following our journey and looking out for us along the way.

Having had gin for breakfast it made perfect sense to have beer for elevenses. Unsworth's Yard is tucked away near the priory in

Gin for breakfast – purely in the interests of science, obviously

Cartmel and just behind the world famous L'Enclume restaurant. The yard is named after the Unsworth family and there's been an Unsworth in residence since 1922. Now a microbrewery, the place has gone through various incarnations, including being a petrol station and the local car repair centre.

From having 4 wagons and a fleet of taxis the business gradually wound down through the 1970s and '80s, and things weren't looking good. But following the arrival of L'Enclume in 2002 things in the village began to turn around. The restaurant began attracting visitors and the owners were keen to work with local businesses as much as they possibly could. Today, L'Enclume even has its own nearby farm and in total directly employs 94 people, as well as sourcing beer and cheese from the village producers.

The Unsworths began by building up their off-licence business and working directly with importers rather than distributors to bring in new and unusual wines and spirits from around the world. The yard was rebuilt, creating a pretty space with the shops surrounding it selling specialist wines, cheeses and breads – honestly, what's not to love?

The problem was they still had one unit spare and weren't quite sure what to do with it. Then, after several drinks celebrating their father's birthday in February 2011, the idea of a microbrewery came about. They didn't rush in. Oh no. They went to visit one microbrewery before they bought all the kit to launch their own. It wasn't until they were on their way home with a van full of secondhand mash tubs that they realised that they didn't know how to make beer.

It's said that the first damson stones were brought back from Damascus during the crusades (hence the name)

Undaunted, Peter went off to work at 3 Peaks Brewery in Settle for 5 weeks to see how it was done, and in January 2012 they produced the first Unsworth's brew, which immediately sold out in the local pubs. Since then they've been perfecting their art but have consistently produced top-notch beer which has an excellent local reputation, and they have remained truly independent throughout, with every single pint still brewed on the premises in Cartmel.

Fearing I may have imbibed too much alcohol the previous day I was all for politely declining all but the tiniest of samples. I put my notebook away, nipped to the loo, and when I emerged Karen was propped up at the bar with a glass of Last Wolf in her hand, ironically looking rather sheepish. As this trip was all about working together I did the honourable thing and joined her.

As we sampled the brews Peter showed us around the tiny yard, which is full of chairs and tables. Along one wall they're growing hops so visitors can see what it looks like before it's turned into beer, and there's a beautiful fountain in the centre made of slate from the local quarry where Peter previously worked, and he was really keen to point out what an open, friendly and welcoming space it is.

'Even if you haven't bought anything from the cheese or bread shops, or even us,' he smiles, 'you're still welcome to come and use the chairs for your packed lunch'.

A local long-distance cycling route, the Morecambe Bay Cycleway, passes through the village and, having visited during the summer months in particular, I can vouch for the fact that the yard has a great atmosphere and is regularly full of folks enjoying the outdoors, eating their sandwiches and usually enjoying a beer or two in the sunshine.

Talking of sunshine, the clouds had finally cleared so we seized the opportunity to head off. As there had been a lot of heavy rain and as Karen was still having trouble with the waterproofness (is that even a word?) of her boots, we opted to keep to the roads. I'm really not comfortable at all with road walking and the route out of Cartmel was particularly busy. Thankfully most cars made a decent effort to avoid us, but one 4x4 raced past at very high speed giving us barely an inch of breathing room – why do people do that? I'm really not sure quite what they were trying to prove.

As we paused for a tea and biscuit break (or a tea and strawberry laces break in my case) we put the rucksacks down next to each other and finally realised why Karen couldn't make her rucksack look as small and neat as mine: it turns out she has a different, larger, rucksack. As we'd both been given our rucksacks by Berghaus several years earlier as prizes for being their monthly blogger, and as both rucksacks were identical colours, we'd assumed they were the same, but no, Karen's was significantly larger. Clearly Berghaus liked her blogs better than they liked mine. Well fine, then.

The route was gently undulating as we headed from High Newton, over Cartmel Fell and down to our overnight stop at Bowland Bridge. Along this section of the route we noticed there were very few cars until one of us decided to stop and try and take a pee, at which point a rush-hour-style gridlock appeared from nowhere. Over the course of the hike we became adept at the 'speed wee,' and even learned to do it with our back packs on.

En route to Bowland Bridge

Our bed for the night was at the Hare and Hounds in Bowland Bridge, and it was just a short walk from the there to Cowmire Hall. (NB they don't have a visitor centre or any facilities, they are simply local folks producing wonderful products, so please don't go knocking on their door).

Cowmire (pronounced Coomer) Hall is a beautiful old family home built around a Pele Tower dating back to 1500, when raids from the north were very much in vogue, and such towers were quite common in the region. Typically the structures had a ground floor for cattle and one or two upper floors for living, allowing the family and livestock to be protected all in one place. Many of them were built for defensive reasons, but there were also quite a few built for decorative purposes or as demonstrations of wealth. Either way, this one is lovely and one of the last ones to be built, so I was very excited to see it.

We were met by the utterly charming Oliver, who showed us around their damson orchards and explained how the family decided to create a liqueur to stimulate damson production in the Lyth Valley, which is full of the trees. Although there are damsons to be found elsewhere in the UK, those of the Lyth Valley are reputed to be the most juicy and flavoursome. Many of the local farms have damson orchards and there are damson trees lining most of the roads.

Damson Day is still celebrated here each year in the spring, and events are held throughout the local area. The timing of the day coincides with the peak of the stunning white blossom on the trees, which people have been coming to admire for many years. The fruit is put to very good use hereabouts, with jams, chutneys, pies and drinks all being produced locally. When the fruit ripens in September you'll find plenty of roadside stalls selling it, together with a range of homemade goodies.

Cowmire Hall Damson Gin is made using another local gin – Bedrock – and added to it are damsons from Oliver's orchard, plus a little sugar, and that's about it. All the damsons, including those bought locally, are frozen before being steeped in the gin. Oliver keeps a plentiful supply of fruit in the freezer, enabling him to maintain year-round production and to continue producing even during years when the crops aren't so good (damsons tend to blossom quite early in the year and are, therefore, very susceptible to spring frosts).

They sell the gin through a range of local outlets and also supply

Fortnum and Mason – not bad for a tiny orchard where all the
steeping and bottling takes place in a small outbuilding roughly the
size of a double garage.

Back at the hotel our rooms were wonderful, with sumptuous
roll-top baths and enormous comfortable beds. But for me the very
best thing was the pie and chips on the menu in the restaurant.
You know how it is when, after a long hike and with no disrespect
whatsoever to L'Enclume, a 6-course taster menu of perfectly
presented morsels piled in the middle of a plate just isn't going to
cut it. I needed pie, I needed chips, and I definitely needed a pint or
so of gravy, all washed down with a further pint – of local ale! And
I wasn't disappointed. (Honestly, as I've typed this I've just googled
them to check a spelling and seen photos of their pie and chips which
someone has uploaded, and I very nearly licked the laptop screen!)

In the interests of full disclosure we also discovered Tirril whisky
while we were there – a Cumbrian brew which had not previously
been on our list. We did try some, only for the sake of the book,
obviously, because I'm nothing if not thorough when it comes to my
research. It was a perfectly lovely brew but, even if we had known
about it when we were planning the route, it's made all the way over
in Appleby, which is a heck of a dogleg. If you're in the area Appleby
is a beautiful town and well worth a visit but, like many of our other
producers, the brewery and distillery are in a large shed in their back
garden and they are not set up for visitors.

I'd like to say it was because we'd had a long couple of days that
we both turned in early, but frankly we're a pair of lightweights and

we needed to be up bright and early the next day. Plus I always think that when you've paid good money for a bed you should spend the maximum amount of time possible in it. Well, that's my excuse anyway. I then did what all married folks do when they finally get an enormous comfortable bed to themselves – I lay diagonally across it, hogged all the covers and drifted off to sleep.

Karen

After a breakfast of porridge with double cream (hiking has its distinct advantages) we just had time for a demo of a magic colour-changing gin. The blue hue of Sharish Blue Magic Gin turns to pink when mixed with tonic. We couldn't just leave the drink sitting there so we both plunged in with straws for our first ever breakfast time G&T.

Then it was on with all the waterproofs to walk the mile down the hill to Peter at Unsworth's Brewery, making our way to the shopfront via a courtyard bedecked with hops.

Peter's grandfather, Ernest, started the Unsworth family business rolling in 1922 with a haulage and garage concern on the site of today's Unsworth's Yard. He'd always been an enterprising soul; as a teenager he used to buy petrol in drums and sell it to folk in the valley who had cars.

'Grandad's business did very well,' said Peter, 'but about 15 years ago things started to tail off and we knew we'd have to change course.'

Peter and his brother David have transformed the struggling business into Unsworth's Yard, a food and drink paradise which includes Unsworth's Brewery, Cartmel Cheeses and Hot Wines, which stocks an extensive range of wines and spirits from all over the world.

'I hadn't even made a home brew when we started this', Peter told us, 'but we thought that other people do it, therefore we can.'

There followed an extremely steep learning curve to master the brewer's art. Since the very first brew was launched on the public in January 2012, the brewery has produced almost half a million pints.

'I still get a thrill from seeing my beer when I go into a pub,' said Peter. 'We are very proud of what we have achieved.'

If time had been on our side, I'd have liked nothing more than to pick up some bread and cheese from the shop next door and sit down in the lovely courtyard to slowly savour a couple of beers. Peter was generously about to pull us as many tasters as we fancied.

I decided to try Last Wolf, a red-brown ale which turned out to be smooth, rich and malty. The beer is named after a local legend which has it that the last wolf in England was killed in nearby Humphrey Head in 1390. On our way I had noticed that the weathervane on top of Cartmel Priory was in the shape of a wolf's head. The legend goes on...

Ahead lay a further 8 miles to get us to Bowland Bridge, our next stopover for the night. But as we tumbled out of Unsworth's Yard (we never did master a steady walking gait when we first heaved the packs on) I wouldn't have cared if someone had said we had 20 miles to go; for I had spotted *blue sky.*

We ambled along the lanes leading out of Cartmel, the drivers passing by at a respectful speed and distance, until one chap roared by in a 4x4, forcing us into the hedgerow where I succumbed to a nettle attack.

I was much happier with the fit of my backpack today. Although as we'd left our accommodation that morning the owner had snapped a photo of us walking away, and when I saw it I still thought my pack looked skewed, and by the various protruding angles you would have sworn I was carrying a dead body. Still, I was comfortable. And things got even better when we stopped for a cuppa and dumped our packs by a gate, and a sudden realisation dawned: after trying to compete for days with Beth's packing, which resulted in a rather neat-looking lump on her back, I knew it was never going to happen for me. Because *her pack was much smaller than mine.* I have no idea why we'd failed to spot it before. I was carrying a 60+15 litre volume pack. Beth's was a 50+10. We'd just assumed that as they'd both been gifts to us from the same company, in the same colours and model, that they were the same size. No, mine was bigger.

'After all that messing!' I said. 'Oh well, Berghaus obviously loved me best.'

It was destined to be a 'good pack day.' Whether I was buoyed up by my discovery that I no longer had to struggle to match Beth's pack prowess, or whether I had simply refitted my own pack in a much better fashion, I don't know. But every so often during our 8-mile walk I had the strangest feeling that my pack had become weightless. I could have skipped along.

Intermittent sunshine and showers accompanied us as we made our way towards Cowmire Hall, where Oliver Barratt was going to tell us all about his damson gin.

Damsons have a special place in my heart, actually, as they fire up vivid memories of childhood, reminding me of my Nan who would make damson crumble as I rushed to drag a chair and clamber up to help. We'd have the crumble with custard and swirl everything into a deep pink pool of juice and fruit. Maybe some of you have similar memories, and of the damson stone game that followed? I didn't realise at the time but damson stones can be a devil to remove, so the fruit was often cooked with the stones in, which made way for a little game: we would save the stones from our portion of crumble and then count them to tell us what we'd be when we grew up: *Tinker, tailor, soldier, sailor, rich man, poor man, beggar man, thief.*

Westmorland Damsons are small, deep-purple plums with a greenish-gold pulp, and although probably not a treat to be enjoyed raw, they really come into their own when baked or steeped or cooked down into a juicy and luscious jam. They grow in the Lyth and Winster valleys, south west of Kendal, and people used to flock to the valleys in droves to see the splendid sea of springtime white blossom on the trees. In September when the fruit ripened, the trucks would head in from Yorkshire and Lancashire to collect the fruit destined for jam-making factories.

But then, just a few decades ago, we nearly lost the Westmorland Damson for good. Fruit gathering costs, combined with tumbling prices and a growth in mass-produced food, saw this little damson falling out of favour.

Fortunately, a few determined locals simply refused to stand by

and watch the fruit and its stunning floral displays slowly vanish from the valleys, and in 1996 the Westmorland Damson Association was formed, with the aim of saving the orchards and encouraging folk to create damson products.

In response, they rolled their sleeves up, and now there is damson jam, jelly and chutney. Pickles, pies and ice cream. Chocolate, cheese and bread. Each year, producers gather on Damson Day, held in April, offering customers a sea of damson delights.

Oliver Barratt and his wife Victoria, of Cowmire Hall, also wanted to do their bit to stimulate the damson economy. They put their heads together and came up with the idea of making damson gin.

From small beginnings in their kitchen when they began steeping damsons with sugar and London Dry Gin in a sweet jar, they converted a farm building into a damson gin cellar and upgraded somewhat to a 600-litre tank.

Oliver showed us around his orchard and we wandered through the damson-laden trees, before heading towards the hub of operations, the gin cellar.

We looked up as Oliver pointed out the pele tower. These thick-walled stone buildings were built in and around the Lake District mainly in the 1500–1600s to withstand sieges and ward off invasion from the Scots. We strained to look up at the roof of the tower – the lookout, a place for firing arrows and launching missiles.

Oliver needed to regain our attention. 'In here,' he motioned, as the wooden door to his cellar creaked open, revealing the gleaming silver tanks, freezers stuffed with damsons and lots of bottles.

On the whole, it's what's inside a bottle that counts. But I'd been surprised on this trip to find that I'd been rather taken by some of the bottle designs chosen by the individual producers. They were definitely something I'd want on show in my home, rather than stuff in a kitchen cupboard. Now, as we approached a distillery or headed towards a pub or cafe to meet the next producer, I was almost looking forward to checking out the packaging as much as tasting the drink. Almost.

Cowmire Hall Gin comes in a simple, tall, clear, wine-shaped bottle, so the ruby-red gin is very much on show. I liked the understated off-white, vintage-style label with its minimal writing and simple sketch of Cowmire Hall.

We waved our goodbyes to Oliver and strolled the easy mile into Bowland Bridge.

I've always been drawn to moving water; rivers, streams and the sea rather than lakes. So as we arrived in Bowland Bridge and Beth suggested dumping our packs by the River Winster to partake in a snifter of Kin Toffee Vodka and chocolate truffles (a gift from Judith), I was all for it.

We twisted open the cap on our vodka, and attacked the chocolate box with far more vigour than either task warranted, and we sat and savoured. The water by our feet bubbled and gurgled. It was incredibly relaxing. I agree wholeheartedly with the marine biologist Wallace J. Nichols, who in his book, *Blue Mind*, shows us how the sight, sound, feel and even smell and taste of water can affect us on a deep level. He even goes as far as to suggest that being near water makes us happier, calmer and more emotionally healthy. As long as he doesn't include rain...

Seriously, when I think about it, water has shaped many of my decisions. I have made conscious life choices to live by the sea or a river whenever I could. In addition, I'll always try to live somewhere where I can avoid experiencing huge amounts of rain. Sometimes, of course, you're not free to choose. But when you can...

Later, as we packed up and crossed the bridge to head to our accommodation, a chap cycling towards us said, 'Ah! Are you on the Spirit Trail?'

'Yes!'

'Saw you on Twitter!' he yelled, as he wobbled away.

Spirit/liqueur info sheet

Product	Cowmire Hall Damson Gin
Category	Liqueur 26% ABV
Who makes it?	Oliver and Victoria Barrett
When did it start production?	1998
Where is it made?	Cowmire Hall, Bowland Bridge
Key ingredients	Bedrock Gin, sugar, damsons
Where can I buy it?	Fortnum & Mason's, throughout UK For full list of stockists visit http://www. damsonginsupplier.co.uk/stockists.html http://www.cowmire.co.uk/stockists.php
Best way to drink it	On its own as a delicious apéritif or liqueur **Damson Gin Sling** Dilute with three parts of cold lemonade and serve with mint, lemon and cucumber.

Oi, that's my juniper bush!

By train	There are no trains from Bowland Bridge to Kendal but Kendal has 2 stations – Oxenholme on the West Coast Mainline and Kendal station in the centre of town
By bus	There are plenty of local buses serving Kendal throughout the year – search South Lakeland buses for up to date timetables
By bike	No Sustrans routes from Bowland Bridge to Kendal but there are a number of quiet country lanes
By car	From Bowland Bridge follow Smithy Lane and Totter Bank through Crosthwaite, then continue on along Underbarrow Road and down into Kendal along Greenside. There are several car parks in the town centre
On foot	From Cowmire we followed the road to Broad Oak then picked up the bridle track around to Row. From there we followed the road to Pinfold Hill then along to Bridgsteer. We then took the public footpath from Crag Mollet to Barrowfield then up and over Scout Scar via Hodgson's Leap before rejoining the road down into Kendal

Distance = 8 miles

DAY FOUR: Bowland Bridge to Kendal

Beth

Peeling ourselves away from the comfortable beds we headed off on our journey towards Kendal. Karen did have a temporary sulk in the doorway of the pub and refuse to come out when an unforecast rain shower blew through, but the sun quickly brightened everything up, Karen included.

After a mile or so I realised that I'd left my walking pole at Oliver's place, but we decided to press on and persuade Steve to pop and collect it and meet me with it in Kendal. During our walk we'd both realised we were carrying far too much in our backpacks, and figured we could hand over all our excesses – plus some of the very kind gifts and drinks we'd been given along the way – which led to Steve gaining the nickname 'Gin Sherpa' for the duration of our hike.

Road walking may be monotonous but at least it's easy and requires very little in the way of navigation, leaving us free to chat about our families and places we'd visited around the world. As an ex-flight attendant married to an ex-pilot, Karen could beat me hands down on that – although she's still never been to Scotland.

I learned a lot from Karen's many adventures – I confess I don't have much wanderlust in me and am very much a home girl. I love exploring the UK, but a fear of flying and an intense dislike of the crowds at airports, coupled with the love I have for our campervan Delores, mean I'm unlikely to ever visit most of the amazing places she has been, or witness the spectacular sights she's seen. On the flip side, she's never experienced Haggis Nachos, so it's maybe not all one sided (the Royal Hotel in Campbeltown on the Kintyre peninsula, if you're wondering – trust me, it's worth the trip for the nachos alone!)

Today the route was mainly off road and along nice, well-drained, limestone tracks and trails. We cut around the back of Whitbarrow Scar and, as we were crossing the next valley towards Scout Scar, we passed a number of roadside honesty shops full of damsons and damson treats, but we simply couldn't carry anything more.

We paused for lunch on the steps of the village hall in Brigsteer,

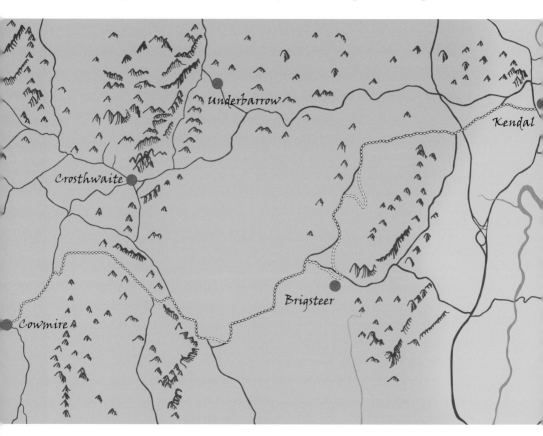

which was very lovely but would definitely have benefited from a few benches. Have you ever noticed that in some places there's an absolute glut of benches (like along the prom at Grange-over-Sands) and in other places, where you could really use a bench, there's not one to be found? I know that in some towns the councils have removed the benches to deter unsavoury groups of folks from congregating but, as I peered around quiet little Brigsteer, I couldn't imagine that was the issue here.

Our route now took us up and over 'juniper central' (Scout Scar) and down into Kendal. Prior to our trip I'd met up with Mike from South Lakes Ecology, who told me all I needed to know about juniper. He said that, like the damsons, juniper grows right across the UK, but some of the best juniper is to be found in Cumbria, where it merrily grows on the limestone.

Actually, it turns out juniper isn't all that fussy and will grow on a whole variety of different soils, but wherever it grows and whatever it does, it takes a long time. It takes two winters to germinate, and the bushes then grow very slowly, living for around 250 years. Juniper berries take two years to ripen, meaning that on every mature female juniper bush you'll see ripened black berries alongside new green berries.

The bushes are generally pretty low to the ground (under 3m), making them perfect for surviving on windy fells, where an upland project with Cumbria Wildlife Trust has recently replanted 15 hectares of juniper across the county. It also turns out they are useful for a lot of things besides the production of gin, though that is clearly its most important contribution to modern life.

Juniper makes an excellent natural nursery for other species. Because it grows low to the ground, and because it's the last thing even the local sheep will eat, other species such as willow, ash and birch seed within it and grow up through it – we spotted this many

times as we made our way over Scout Scar. There's even juniper planted 650m up on Skiddaw and it's doing really well, apparently.

A recent study that Mike was involved with demonstrated that over 40 different animal species relied solely on juniper, and for dozens more it was a vital part of their diet, so it's also a crucial part of our nation's ecology and the reason that replanting is such an important issue. It's quite safe for humans to eat, though only in tiny amounts, and is excellent when tossed into a casserole alongside venison or lamb.

'How do I know if it's juniper?' I asked Mike, worried that I might eat the wrong thing and inadvertently poison myself and Karen; I didn't want to poison my new friend so early in the hike, it really wouldn't look good.

'Easy,' he says, 'squeeze it and if it smells like gin then it's juniper.'

Good point. I may never be a botanist but I can certainly spot the smell of gin.

As we were crossing Scout Scar we put that to the test and squished a few berries before tentatively eating them. They (and we) were thankfully absolutely fine, but I'm not sure I'd ever be tempted to eat a bowlful.

Our legs were tiring and in an effort to keep our spirits up I promised Karen that there were some excellent places for cake in Kendal.

'You can't buy me with cake,' she said, then paused for a moment. 'Wait, did you say coffee and walnut?'

Dropping down into Kendal felt odd for me – I live not too far away and have visited the town many times, but I've never yomped along the high street with a full pack on my back before. In the more 'outdoorsy' towns such as Ambleside or Keswick a couple of hikers with huge backpacks are pretty common, but in Kendal they're more of a rarity and we did attract a few odd glances.

Our bed for the night was at Kendal Hostel – we both had pretty old memories of hostels and had needed to double check with Jan, the owner, that we wouldn't require sleeping bags. She assured us that we didn't and that these days hostels were rather more modern.

As we waited for the hostel to open we made ourselves comfortable in Brew Brothers and treated ourselves to some of the fine cake I'd promised Karen earlier. In a world full of big chains it's a joy to find small independent places like Brew Brothers offering superb coffee and a huge range of local cakes and biscuits in a lovely cosy atmosphere. The shop is small but comfortable, with a serving counter laden with all manner of sinful treats. I could see it was going to be hard dragging Karen away from this.

Kendal Hostel is right next to the Brewery Arts Centre (another of my favourite haunts) and Jan welcomed us with a beaming smile. I think my best description of the interior would be comfortably curious. The building is Grade II listed and is packed full of all sorts of quirky furniture and ornaments, with a huge woodburner in the middle of the lounge. Everything is spotlessly clean and, as a Blue Badge guide, Jan is one of the most knowledgeable folk I've met and brims over with enthusiasm as she tells you about all the things you can see and do in the area.

She led us along the winding corridors to our room and I had mild concerns about whether I'd ever find my way back out again.

Think this is a juniper, or is it a yew?!

*'Juniper Central',
aka Scout Scar*

We passed the huge kitchen (crammed with enough gadgetry and utensils to keep Gordon Ramsay happy) and the dining room next door, where we could join the happy throng or hide in a corner and eat in peace.

After a long hike neither of us felt like cooking, so after a pint and a pizza in Brewery Arts we headed out to meet Mike Pennington, the man behind the greenest drink you ever did see.

Mike and his wife Annie own Burgundy's wine bar in Kendal and are the brains behind Kendal Mint Cake Liqueur and Lakeland Moon Gin. Sir Edmund Hillary famously took Kendal Mint Cake to the summit of Everest and it has been synonymous with Kendal and outdoor adventure ever since. Mike was born and raised in the town – in fact when he moved across town his family thought he'd emigrated – and he has fond memories of making mint cake with his grandad in their kitchen. Back then every family had their own recipe, handed down from generation to generation.

Fast forward a few decades and Mike, who loves making new things, was bored one Saturday evening and decided to try making a cocktail using Kendal Mint Cake. He started making small batches of it for family and friends, and by 2014 Annie was selling it in the

Christmas markets, where it went down a storm. Realising they had something good on their hands, they decided to do things properly and spent eight months designing the bottles and labels and putting the finishing touches to the liqueur before having a 'proper launch' in August 2015.

It's still made locally with a variety of local ingredients. As Mike proudly puts it, 'it's made without an accountant,' by which he means that he found the very best ingredients and methods to produce the perfect drink and built the brand around that. When you take a sip you will experience 3 distinct stages: mint, chocolate and warmth. Always in that order.

The most noticeable thing about the drink is its distinctive green colour. It is vivid, luxurious and, most importantly in a competitive drinks market, it stands out and will brighten the spirits shelf behind any bar. The colour is not a curious by-product of the production of the liqueur but a deliberate addition – it's known as 'Kendal Green' and is closely tied into the wool-producing history of the town. The original Kendal Green was a hardwearing woollen fabric worn by the Kendal archers at the battle of Agincourt, and Mike has used it to perfect effect to colour a drink that is gloriously unique.

Following the popularity of the liqueur, Mike and Annie ventured into gin production. Lakeland Moon Gin is a proper London Dry Gin made using local juniper harvested under the full moon (in accordance with the practices of biodynamic farming), plus 6 other botanicals. As with the Mint Cake Liqueur, Mike insisted on using only the very best of ingredients and cut his margins in order to make the best drink he could for a sensible price. It's not cheap but then life is too short to drink cheap gin.

There's a recipe card of quirky and delicious cocktails in the bar (and on their website), and following our chat, with our notebooks now safely stashed, Mike and Annie proceeded to tempt us with half a dozen or so of their most inventive. There was the exotic and mysterious Love Potion No. 2 (Lakeland Moon Gin mixed with prosecco), the crisp and clean Sir Edmund Hillary (an ice-cold shot of Mint Cake Liqueur in an ice-cold glass with a frosting of icing sugar), and the newly invented and provisionally named 'Grouse in the Grass,' which shouldn't work but actually does – Kendal Mint Cake Liqueur mixed with a decent single malt such as Talisker. I know, as a huge fan of good single malts, it sounds wrong to me too. Very wrong. But it tastes great, you'll just have to trust me on that one.

I think the most telling thing about our wonderful evening with Mike and Annie was the selfie we took at the end. Each time we met someone we posed with them for a photo to use on social media, and looking back on them now they are all crisp, clean, sharp and shiny,

with the exception of this one. The one we took at the end of the evening with 'Minty Mike' is wonky, fuzzy, blurry and poorly lit. Still, you can't deny we all look happy. Must have been the entertaining conversation...

Karen

After several gin-packed days of sniffing, tasting, and begging for refills, we decided that our mission for the day would be to find some juniper. Fortunately, Beth had recently met with a chap from South Lakes Ecology who had given her some tips on where we were likely to find plenty of the bushes. Scout Scar was one such place and we were due to hike through it today on our way to Kendal.

We duly made our way around Whitbarrow Scar and ascended to Scout scar.

I wasn't expecting much. The only information I'd gleaned online about Scout Scar was that it was a great place to fill time before heading to the 'fells proper' or 'tickable hills,' as some perceptive chap had called them.

Scout Scar isn't difficult to get to and you'd never call it high, but if you're looking to go a little wild (and who isn't) by immersing yourself in peace and greenery, then Scout Scar fits the bill. Which is surprising considering its close proximity to Kendal.

Up here it was so open, so fresh, utterly tranquil, and – for me anyway – there was a huge sense of escapism. I loved the level ground; I could plonk my feet down on the paths and tracks, with barely a thought to watching my footing, and look up and out over the landscape.

A fellrunner whooshed by in a rush of gorgeous aftershave. I turned and watched the bright dot of his orange top getting smaller and smaller as he ran further away, dodging among the clumps of bracken. I wanted to do that. One day...

Beth came to a sudden halt. 'Look! There!'

Just ahead, the landscape was dotted with green islands of spiky-leaved bushes, looking very much like the rosemary in my garden. These bushes, though, were studded with berries like blackcurrants. It looked like we'd found our juniper.

'Are we sure?' I asked. 'How do we know it's juniper?'

'Taste it,' said Beth.

'After you.'

'Let's squish it.'

The scent was unmistakeably gin. This was probably going to go down as the best bit of foraging I'd ever done. It was some time before we moved on, only the lure of the buildings of Kendal in the distance pulling us onwards.

Over the next hour or so, the enticing glimpses of Kendal got closer...then further away. Finally, we set our weary feet onto the high street and sought our bed for the night at Kendal Hostel.

I had never stayed in a youth hostel before. I had vague memories of a friend telling me years ago that she'd had an amazing time, as the place she stayed in was right in the middle of town, and the room rate was so reasonable that she'd had spare cash to spend in said town. It was her parting shot that struck fear into my heart:

'I hit the town as soon as my chores were done.'

'Chores? What, like drying your boots and stuff?' I'd said.

'No! Youth hostel chores. Everyone pitches in.'

I had visions of myself before the kitchen sink, beads of sweat dripping off my face into the sudsy water as I scoured an entire hostel's-worth of pots and pans. Still, if I played my cards right, Beth would probably be put to work scrubbing the outside toilets.

I'd already had my fingers burned during a brief 'youth hostel' googling session before I set off on this trip, when up popped the youth hostel in Ottawa, a former jail of which the top floor was the former death row. Then there was the hostel just outside Stockholm, notable for being where Sweden's last execution took place. I leapt away from my laptop as though I'd been scalded.

Still, this was the soft and genteel Lake District ... wasn't it?

I was relieved to find that Kendal Hostel really was slap bang in the middle of town, with every coffee shop, restaurant and store you might ever need just a few paces down the road. As it was cold and wet and we only had flimsy flip flops for evening wear I was incredibly happy with the location. We had to go out again later to meet Minty Mike in a bar in town that evening, so we wouldn't be flip-flopping with frozen toes for long.

We walked up the steps into Kendal Hostel. My first impression

Scout Scar. 'If you squish a berry and it smells of gin ...'

was that it was beautifully warm, with cosy sofas, and owner Jan rushing forth to shower us with offers of warm drinks and effusive kindness. No mention of chores yet.

Our room was spotlessly clean with plenty of room for manoeuvre, which matters when you've got your home on your back.

We didn't have much time to play with before meeting Mike and his wife, Annie, in Burgundy's Wine Bar, so the fact that the Brewery Arts Centre was located just behind the hostel was certainly handy; turns out it serves fabulous cold beers and terrific pizza.

We were getting to know each other better. Beth was shocked that I hadn't quite twigged that Whitehaven (of which she's inordinately fond) was on the coast. I argued that it was nowhere near as outrageous as the fact that she'd never had a Gregg's sausage roll. Now't so strange as folk.

Fortunately, we reached the door of Burgundy's just as Beth began to tackle me on my cake intake; she was still sore from an hour before when we'd rushed out for a few provisions. She had whizzed around the minimart in 30 seconds flat and was eager to snuggle back into the hostel to make the most of the little spare time we had, whereas I hadn't even begun to locate the shelves of chocolate, never mind selected the three bars I had in mind.

But now, as we pushed open the bar door, our thoughts turned to tastings.

We settled around a table tucked at the back of the room just before Minty Mike and Annie arrived. Locals were quick to label Mike with the moniker after he put his mind to creating a liqueur from Kendal Mint Cake, the snack which famously powered Sir Edmund Hillary to the summit of Everest.

If you've never tasted Kendal Mint Cake, it's an intense hit of pure pepperminty sugar.

Mike is the owner of Burgundy's, and with his cocktail skills and the help of his customers as eager tasters, he stirred, mixed, poured and fine-tuned until he realised he'd got it right.

The drink before me, sitting in a shot glass rimmed with lemon sugar, was a bright emerald green. The rim frosting is to suggest the snow-capped peak of Everest. Mike had wasted no time in rolling up his sleeves and creating a couple of Edmund Hillary's for us to try. I took a sip and my mouth filled with a cool, fresh burst of peppermint.

Mike had already disappeared again behind the bar and was mixing up a couple of Minthoppers.

While the Edmund Hillary was bold and vibrant, the Minthopper was velvety and smooth, with its double cream and flaked chocolate. If you're partial to those deliciously chocolate-covered peppermints then it's no big stretch at all to try drinking them. I challenge you not to groan with pleasure.

'Now. You've got to try it with whisky,' said Mike, and headed off to the bar again.

Whisky? I struggled to imagine that adding a dash of whisky to the liqueur was going to work. That wouldn't work at all. But of course I had to try it.

'Beth! You've just got to try this!'

'In a minute.'

Beth had wrapped her fingers tightly around her Minthopper, almost as if she didn't trust me not to try and wriggle my straw in there. As if!

I decided I was a little bit in love with mint.

Did you know that the flavours you enjoy supposedly give hints to your personality? Apparently, mint lovers are the coolest kids on the block; they're also quite soft and sweet but a little on the anxious side with a tiny touch of jittery. I can go with that.

I also like the oaky flavours in scotch and that apparently means I'm sure as hell likely to have two days' worth of stubble, every day. I can go with that too.

Mike and Annie also make Lakeland Moon Gin, which is made with juniper berries from the Lakeland Fells plucked under a full moon.

Mike was up to his cocktail tricks again and whipped up a Love Potion; there was gin, sugar and lemon juice, all topped up with prosecco and a thin drizzle of grenadine. A stream of bubbles rose gently to the top of the glass from the warming red glow at the bottom.

We flip-flopped back through Kendal to the hostel, well-fortified with delicious spirits.

'Last one back does the chores!'

Less than half an hour later our room was filled with gentle snores.

Spirit/liqueur info sheet

Product	Kendal Mint Cake Liqueur Lakeland Moon Gin
Category	Liqueur 24 % ABV Gin: London Dry Gin 42.1% ABV
Who makes it?	Pennington's Premium Spirits And Liqueurs
When did it start production?	Kendal Mint Cake Liqueur, 1990 Lakeland Moon Gin, 2017
Where is it made?	Kendal
Key ingredients	**Liqueur**: pure British grain alcohol, British beet sugar, Penningtons Kendal Mint Cake recipe, natural mint and chocolate flavouring, Lake District pure spring water. All blended into a smooth mint and chocolate liqueur. **Gin**: A blend of wild juniper gathered from the Lakeland Fells under a full moon and selected botanicals, along with Lake district spring water, resulting in a clean London Dry Gin with a smile of sunny orange
Where can I buy it?	https://www.kendalmintcakeliqueur.com/shop/

KENDAL MINT CAKE LIQUEUR

Edmund Hillary
Run lemon over the rim of shot glass.
Dip into sugar.
Fill glass with Kendal Mint Cake
Liqueur, straight from the freezer.

Minthopper
Use a Martini Glass
Run lemon over the rim of the glass
Dip into a mixture of sugar and cocoa
powder
Into a cocktail shaker put:
50ml of Kendal Mint Cake Liqueur
50ml of double cream
6 ice cubes
Shake & strain into Martini Glass
Sprinkle flakes chocolate over the top
Garnish with a sprig of mint

Highgate Hottie
1 1/2oz Shot Glass
1oz of Kendal Mint Cake Liqueur
Float 1/2oz of Sambuca on top
Pop on top 3 coffee beans
Set alight.

Mint Royale
Champagne flute
15mls of Kendal Mint Cake Liqueur
Top up with prosecco
Add a sprig of mint

Pirates of Kendal
Use an 8oz high ball glass
Half fill with ice
25ml of Kendal Mint Cake Liqueur
25ml spiced rum
Fill to top with Coca Cola
Garnish with lemon of glass rim

Captain French
Fill a heavy bottomed whisky tumbler
with ice
Pour over 25ml of Kendal Mint Cake
Liqueur
Follow with 25ml of spiced rum
Stir and add a sprig of mint and a thin
stick of red pepper (optional)

LAKELAND MOON GIN

Martian Moon
50ml Lakeland Moon Gin
25ml Kendal Mint Cake Liqueur
25ml sugar syrup
25ml fresh lime juice
Stir with ice for 2 minutes
Pour into a tall glass
Fill to rim with sparkling
elderflower
Garnish with a twist of unwaxed
lime peel

Moon Martini
60ml Lakeland Moon Gin
20ml Noilly Prat
Shaken not stirred
Serve in a chilled glass
Garnish with a strip of orange
zest

Wordsworth's Wankle
Take a large wine glass
Half fill with ice
50ml Lakeland Moon Gin
Half bottle Fever-Tree Aromatic
Tonic
Add a wedge of pink grapefruit
and 6 blueberries
Stir gently

Poet's Ink
50ml Lakeland Moon Gin
25ml blue curacao
Cocktail cherry
6 cracked ice cubes into a mixing
glass
Add the gin, curacao, stir well
Strain into a chilled cocktail glass
Add cherry for garnish

Love Potion No II
50ml Lakeland Moon Gin
25ml sugar syrup
25ml freshly squeezed lemon juice
Mix and pour into a champagne
flute
Top up with prosecco
Drizzle in a thin line of grenadine

Sponsored by cake and chocolate

By train	Regular service from Kendal station into Windermere
By bus	A number of bus routes connect Kendal and Windermere; please check local timetables for more information
By bike	Sustrans Route 6 runs from Kendal through Windermere to Bowness
By car	From Kendal follow the A591 to Bowness. Parking is limited in the village, particularly during the summer months
On foot	We left Kendal past Plumgarths on the A591 and continued on to Crook. In the village we turned right to follow a local road until we intercepted the Dales Way which we then followed down into Bowness

Distance = 9 Miles

DAY FIVE: Kendal to Windermere

Beth

It's been a long time since I stayed in a hostel and the breakfast chaos caught me on the hop a little at first. I'll confess that I'm not all that sociable first thing in the morning, especially after a night spent sampling Minty Mike's famous cocktails. I prefer a little bit of quiet time to wake my brain up, so to be greeted with half a dozen or so people, all laughing and chatting, was a bit overwhelming, and as soon as I'd grabbed my porridge and coffee I retreated to a corner of the dining room to collect my thoughts. I felt a bit mean really, as everyone was so friendly, but I just needed a few minutes to rid my brain of the last vestiges of Mint Cake Liqueur and focus on the day ahead.

After breakfast Jan kindly showed us a letter from Beatrix Potter which she'd recently bought at auction. To stand there with a letter written by this remarkable woman was quite something. It was in a fragile condition and the loopy handwriting was hard to read in places, but Jan has it well protected and is rightfully very proud of it.

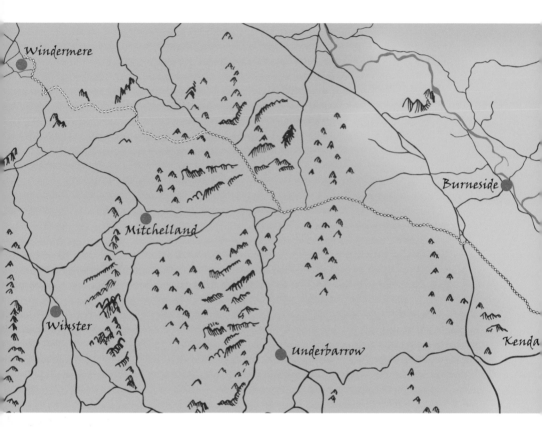

Our route for the day was to be a mixture of tarmac and cross country, and we knew the rain was coming in again so we didn't hang around – we bid Jan a fond farewell and headed out of town.

The long, slow haul up the hill out of town towards Plumgarths was pretty mundane, and the queues of traffic heading down into town were a reminder that the rest of the world was still going about its usual 9–5, while we were heading out onto a rainy hillside. For a fleeting moment I did wonder if a nice, warm, dry office might be a better option today, especially when we reached the 'Windermere 7 Miles' milestone and the rain began to fall, but the feeling soon passed.

Unbeknown to Karen I had a secret stop planned at the start of our journey, but as it involved cake I was pretty sure she'd be okay with it. Ginger Bakers are based in a tiny retail park near Plumgraths roundabout and they are the creators of an enormous range of cakes and bakes. I had my heart firmly set on a slab of their beetroot and berry brownie, and I was quite prepared to sit on the floor and cry like a baby if they didn't have any. Worryingly there was none out on display, but as soon as they saw my bottom lip begin to quiver they scurried off and dug out a few pieces from the kitchen. One of the definite perks of a long-distance hike is the freedom to eat as much chocolate brownie as you can carry – plus I was counting both the beetroot and the berries in this one as at least 2 of my 'five a day'.

When people talk about rain on their holidays not being too bad because 'at least it was warm rain', I have absolutely no idea what they mean. As we continued along the road the rains arrived, so we needed to don our waterproofs again. But because they were 'warm rains,' thanks to some meteorological quirk, we were also boiling hot. I really hate being hot, so while I grouchily stomped along the road muttering assorted oaths, Karen, who is well used to dealing with the hot and sticky climate in Cyprus, raced off ahead. Although she thought it was cold.

We paused under a tree in Crook for a drink and a bite or two of our brownies (who am I kidding, we downed the first one in a few hungry gulps!). As Karen shivered and enjoyed her hot chocolate I opened my waterproof to let some air in and explored the small enclosure surrounding us. It was apparently an 18th-century livestock pen where stray farm animals were kept until their owner could collect them. Momentarily forgetting Karen's dislike of history, I got all excited and started telling her about it, before the look on her face reminded me of the error of my ways. I hadn't realised quite what a history bore I was. Usually I'm walking with Steve, who is equally interested in quirky bits of history, and we enjoy learning about the landscape around us, but that's the fun challenge of a new walking partner – finding things to talk about which won't bore the other person to distraction.

As we pulled the waterproof covers back over the rucksacks a delivery driver who'd been unloading his van nearby offered us a lift. Watching the rain drip off the trees and run down our jackets he must have thought us pretty odd to have refused him. We tried to explain about the Spirit Trail idea but I'm not convinced he understood.

Our plan was to follow the back road out of Crook and then pick up the Dales Way over into Windermere. As usual Karen raced ahead of me up the hill – I have one hill speed and it's slow – but unfortunately I hadn't communicated our turning clearly enough to her and she strode straight past it. I joined forces with a couple of other hikers to call after her, but she was long gone; my only option was to sit tight, wait for her to notice that I was further behind than usual, and come looking for me, which she thankfully did.

There's no denying the fact that the weather through this part of the trek was foul – strong winds and pouring rain. I'd decided against my waterproof trousers as I was hot enough already and, during the brief periods when the rain eased, the strong winds quickly dried me out. Thankfully the Dales Way is well signposted so there weren't too many navigational pauses. When things get grotty in the fells I often resort to singing to keep my spirits up, though it has to be said I have a voice that only the deaf will truly appreciate. As I was deep into what I thought was a particularly rousing rendition of 'Zip a dee do dah, zip a dee ay, My oh my what a wonderful day,' for the first time in the journey Karen lagged behind – I'm not sure if she was avoiding my singing or if the persistent rain was starting to get to her.

That night we were to have an entire cottage to ourselves, thanks to Sally's Cottages, who'd kindly offered to put us up, and as we trudged down from the hillside and through the streets of Windermere we listed all the things we were planning to do – hot baths, hot food, hot drinks and lots and lots of warm, dry clothes.

Arriving at the cottage Karen's fingers were too cold to turn the wheels on the key safe, but we eventually opened the door and, dumping all our wet gear on the mat in the hallway, headed straight out to the Co-op to stock up on goodies. Looking at the contents of our shopping baskets we were either a) going to have to have a LOT of baths and eat a LOT of food that night, or b) have to carry a lot more stuff for the rest of the journey. Luckily our Gin Sherpa was due to visit again that evening to resolve another mix-up with my walking pole, so he could take away some of our over-enthusiastic purchases.

I nipped to the bathroom to run the first of the hot baths and there, on the wall opposite the loo, was a sign reading 'Life is not about waiting for the storm to pass, it's about learning to dance in

the rain.' I keeled over in a fit of giggles but I'm not sure Karen is ready to practice her raindance just yet.

That evening I left Karen to her own devices (literally, she loves her phone) while I headed out to meet some friends in the wonderfully named Crafty Baa just around the corner. Quite predictably I ordered a G&T, while they pumped me for information such as 'What's she like?' 'Have you fallen out yet?' 'How much have you had to drink?' I had to disappoint them by saying that we hadn't fallen out – true, we had our differences, but nothing worth falling out over – so long as I remembered to curtail my historical rants.

When I arrived back at the cottage I spotted the bottle of Gilpin's Gin on the counter with a good measure or two missing, which explained Karen's nice rosy glow as she sat curled up on the sofa. I happen to have a very strict 'don't let your friends drink alone' policy, so I poured myself a large one and joined her. Gilpins is produced by Westmorland Spirits Ltd and although it is now distilled 'down south', the Gilpin family have historic ties with Cumbria going back to 1215. In fact Richard de Gilpin accompanied the Baron of Kendal to Runnymede where the Magna Carta was sealed. As I wallowed in a bit of history Karen was muttering something about botanicals and citrus, but I was starting to doze off – which had nothing to do with Karen and everything to do with being warm, cosy and full of gin.

After a particularly soggy day I was very keen to get to my nice warm, dry bed, while my boots dried out on the radiators downstairs – we even managed to get a load of washing done to reduce our knicker-rinsing obligations for the coming few days. Having an entire cottage to ourselves was an absolute luxury and I was enjoying every single second of it.

Karen

After a lovely warm, snuggly night in Kendal Hostel we waved our goodbyes to super host Jan (who plied us with cakes) and set off to walk to Windermere. It was single file along the narrow and soggy grassy verges of the road which would get us out of town. Beth hates road walking but was remarkably chirpy. With my hood pulled tightly over my head, just nose showing, I'd no idea what she was saying, so maybe I missed the reason for her buoyant mood. It all became clear when she dragged me off-route into Ginger Bakers in search of her beloved beetroot and berry brownies. The morning could have been a complete washout (excuse the pun) when the little tray on the counter allocated to the brownies was completely empty, save a few crumbs. The two absolute angels behind the counter heroically managed to save the day by somehow conjuring up two pieces from the kitchen.

Rain fell steadily as we trudged on. Perfect. I could put my plan into action.

Over the last few days, whenever I'd dripped into any establishment I'd found myself getting just a tad irritated.

Without the rain, there wouldn't be rainbows!

Well, I'd give up a rainbow any day for the sight of that bone-warming yellow orb in the sky.

There's no such thing as bad weather, only bad clothing!

This one does get my goat. I'm pretty sure that originally it was a bit of fun, a sort of little nudge of encouragement to fair-weather hikers and the like who would instantly wimp out at less than perfect conditions. But it's become more than that. It's disparaging. Belittling. 'Not a real hiker then!' As if battling the fury of Mother Nature is a mark of your mettle. Granted, there is poor clothing. There are also plenty of weather conditions when you'd have to be crazy to go out in the hills.

Of course, everyone knows that Cumbria is rainy. It wouldn't be so lush and green otherwise. And *lakey*. And the weather we'd experienced so far was most definitely nowhere near the 'abandon hike' category. But it was very wet and I obviously hadn't prepared myself enough for this.

I had remembered a quote from somewhere that said, 'Much of

our suffering in life is the result of a desire to have reality be different than it actually is'.

I'd never dream of equating a bit of rain with suffering, but it was true. I wasn't annoyed at the rain itself; I can easily cope with that. No, it was because I felt the rain was spoiling my plans. I'd had visions of Beth and I dumping our packs regularly as we paused for

Enjoying the weather(!)

some hot coffee, nestling in amongst the trees and taking in the view. The reality was that most of the time we didn't feel encouraged to stop; our flasks were under several layers of GORE-TEX and there was no view.

And what was causing my annoyance at these circumstances? Me.

So, I gave myself a talking to.

Last night, just as I was drifting off to sleep, I'd decided on my mantra for the following day: *Hiking in the rain can be fun. Embrace the rain.*

Even so, when a van driver took pity on us and offered us a lift, it was with a heavy heart that I declined.

We were due to stay in The Hideaway in Windermere that evening and I didn't know what to expect. Yes, hiking in the rain could be fun, but part of that fun is knowing that at the end of the day, I'd have a warm place to dry off and sleep. Putting on cold, wet hiking socks in the morning should be a capital offence.

A gap opened up between us as we made to join the Dales Way. I hoped that Beth was enjoying some time alone with her thoughts, as I was. Actually, if you crave peace and quiet during your walks then rainy days when folk hole up indoors are some of the best.

I'd been struggling a bit with a book I'm currently writing. As I walked, I mulled it over. The project had started off well, my thoughts spilling onto the paper almost faster than I could scribble, but it had all dried up. I seemed to have hit a brick wall.

I needed space to unravel my mind. It's when I'm out walking that ideas tend to bubble to the surface. As Henry David Thoreau wrote in his journal, 'Methinks that the moment my legs begin to move, my thoughts begin to flow.'

Intriguing signage on the Crook road

And flow they did. But as I couldn't record my gushing thoughts on my phone as I'd normally do, I had to work out some little rhymes to help me remember them.

Squeak, creak, squeak.

My backpack had been playing up, and the squeaking was driving me nuts. I'd tried repacking it to redistribute the load, I'd showered the suspect parts with talcum powder and massaged Vaseline generously into wherever I could squeeze my finger.

Squeak, creak, squeak.

It had been singing the song of its people for days now. I was beginning to suspect that it was actually my body that was creaking.

We ploughed on, to join the Dales Way which would disgorge us neatly into Windermere.

Over the last few days, Beth and I had been pretty relieved to discover that we both hiked at around the same pace. The only exception to this was hills. Beth likes to hunker down for a slow and steady ascent, whereas I prefer to power up them as fast as my little legs and lungs will allow. I don't mind the increased discomfort; I just want it to be shortlived. Watching me going uphill with full backpack is not pretty. You'll see me striving to find the crucial balance between leaning into the hill and leaning so far forward that the weight of the backpack will force a face plant in the mud. It's akin to watching a weeble, one of those roly poly toys from the seventies with the slogan 'Weebles wobble but they don't fall down'. Hopefully.

By the time I near the top, my heart is pounding to the point that I can hear it beating out of my ears.

And this is how we nearly came to lose each other.

'Hills coming up!' spotted Beth. 'Off you go!'

I battled up the first hill only to see another looming, so I kept on.

I breasted the next hill and carried on, lost in my thoughts.

I don't know what made me turn round at one point, but I did and realised that Beth was nowhere to be seen. Nothing for it but to retrace my steps. Luckily, Beth had realised that I'd missed a turning and had stayed put, so it wasn't long before I spotted her forlorn figure in the distance. We hadn't planned for this sort of thing but we should have.

'This way,' she pointed.

'Isn't that a river?'

'No, that's the path.'

The way was soggy, muddy, windy and miserable. As it was impossible to talk much, we knuckled down and carried on. I dreamed of hot chocolate with cream and marshmallows, deep fried mars bars, Cornish pasties and an Epsom salt bath. Though I'd no idea where I was going to get my hands on any of them.

We crossed bubbling fords, waded through heaps of mushy cow dung, and finally descended into Windermere. Beth was singing 'Zip a dee do dah'. I was searching for some hedgerow twine to strangle her with. *Mantra, Karen, mantra.*

Evidently, I'm a terribly lapsed northerner. For most of us our hometown and region are a source of pride and there's nothing wrong with that. When I first moved south I found that folk expected me to eat pies every day and I was happy to oblige. It was the first I'd heard of the north-south divide. When I asked my Dad about it he said not to worry as it was all about beer. Which is why he wouldn't come and visit.

Finally we were in amongst the residential streets of Windermere searching for The Hideaway, our cottage for the night.

A man tumbled out of his house, half-sighted as he squinted in the rain, and nearly ran into us.

'Crikey. Not a day for hiking, girls!'

The Hideaway was a stone terraced cottage tucked in the heart of Windermere village. At the end of the street I could see the awnings of the restaurants and shops. Perfect. Pushing open the door we elbowed and kneed each other as we squeezed both our steaming bodies onto the doormat, and attempted to peel off our soggy layers without taking half of the water of Lakeland into the house with us. We went in to investigate.

'It's *so* stylish. Love it!' I said.

'Yeah, really nicely done.'

'It's got *everything*!'

Heating, wifi, a washing machine, gloriously comfortable beds with fluffy duvets, and a huge – just waiting for me – bath.

'Wait! Shouldn't we nip out to the corner shop before we really settle in?' said Beth.

Why didn't we think of this before stripping off?

Fifteen minutes later and armed with essential provisions – pies, wine, chocolate and bubble bath – we finally closed the door on the outside world.

Matthew Gilpin had generously sent us a bottle of his gin to accompany us on our trip and now – warm, dry and replete in our cosy cottage – it seemed as good a time as any to break into it.

Gilpin's Extra Dry Gin is made at Thames Distillers and, as the name suggests, it doesn't contain any of the sweeter botanicals, and even uses a bitter version of orange.

I'd read that the gin includes sage, as Matthew is fond of the flavour and smell. I'm not, so I was interested to see how that would turn out. When it comes to ordering a drink, though, I'll always opt for the dry version, so the 'extra dry' labelling was appealing.

As I rolled the warming liquid around my tongue I could definitely detect citrus, which I guessed was the bitter orange. It was very smooth with plenty of juniper. I'm sure that a more experienced palate than mine could have detected many more flavours in there, but when it comes down to it, all that matters is whether you like it or not. And I most definitely did.

'That's it. I'm never leaving this place. Never. You can carry on without me.'

Beth knows how to make a grown woman cry.

'There's a giant pasty shop on our way to the ferry tomorrow.'

We holed away in the toasty cottage until forced out the next morning by a pressing itinerary and a giant pasty. Onwards and upwards...

Spirit/liqueur info sheet

Product	Gilpin's Westmorland Extra Dry Gin
Category	London Dry Gin 47% ABV
Who makes it?	Matthew Gilpin
When did it start production?	2012
Where is it made?	Thames Distillery, London
Key ingredients	Made from pure English grain spirit pot-distilled with just eight botanicals. Juniper, sage, borage, lime, coriander, lemon, bitter orange, angelica root.
Where can I buy it?	http://www.gilpinsgin.com/buy

Best way to drink it?

Gilpin's Gibson
(dry martini made with
silverskin onions)
75ml Gilpin's Gin;
5ml Noilly Prat;
Silver cocktail onions

Gin and Tonic
Fill a balloon glass full of ice
60% Gilpin's Westmorland
Gin
40% Fever-Tree Original
Tonic
Slice of lemon garnish or
orange twist

Ultimate Gin & Tonic
50ml Gilpin's Gin
100ml tonic water
Lemon wedge or orange
twist

Red Snapper
(gin Bloody Mary)
35ml Gilpin's Gin
100ml tomato juice
10ml fino sherry
Tabasco, Worcestershire
sauce & horseradish

Martini
75ml Gilpin's Gin
5ml Noilly Prat
Olives
Lemon or orange twist

Negroni
25ml Gilpin's Gin
25ml Campari
25ml red vermouth

Plain sailing

By train	No train service – thanks to Wordsworth & friends campaigning against it
By bus	A number of bus routes connect Windermere to Ambleside, please check local timetables for more information
By bike	Sustrans Route 6 runs from Windermere through Bowness to Ambleside
By car	From Windermere continue along the A591 to Ambleside. There are various car parks in the town but your best bet for a space is the one next to Rothay Park
By boat	Windermere Lake Cruises run a regular service throughout the year from Bowness to Ambleside.
On foot	Walk down into Bowness and cross to Far Sawry on the ferry. From there follow the broad track leading north along the lake shore, past Wray Castle, then onto the road, through Clappersgate and into Ambleside.

Distance = 10 miles

DAY SIX: Windermere to Ambleside

Beth

After enjoying a luxurious long, hot shower I left Karen fussing around her rucksack while I went out for a short look around Windermere. I often wonder whether when people book their hotel in the town they realise they're a mile or so from the lake. Bowness-on-Windermere is the town on the lake shore, whereas Windermere is a mile or so uphill away from the lake.

Windermere village is another of those lovely places where the big name chains don't dominate the high street. There are plenty of quirky little shops and businesses to explore, selling everything from paintings to shoes. In the window of the Northern Line gift shop I noticed a 'Gin O'Clock' clock, which reminded me I'd better get back to Karen – I had by now established a strong Pavlovian connection between 'gin' and 'Karen'.

Before we left the village we popped in to say hello to Anthony in Windermere Wines, with the idea of getting some photos of the wide range of local spirits he sells. He surprised us with 2 small bottles of

Mint Cake Liqueur left for us by Minty Mike – a delightful gift and definitely something our Gin Sherpa would need to collect from us that evening.

The route from Windermere to Bowness is an easy mile or so downhill – honestly it's not far at all – but along the way we still managed to find another off-licence rammed to the rafters with local spirits, including one we'd not yet discovered, Gingerbread Vodka. The owner kindly offered us a sample (it was worrying how drinking spirits before lunch was quickly becoming our norm). We were both mightily impressed, although I don't have much of a sweet tooth where drinks are concerned, so I'm not sure I'd manage more than a few sips, but the gingerbread really came through and stopped it becoming too sickly.

Because we don't want to leave anyone out if we can help it I tracked down Dave Hall, the man behind the vodka, after our walk to find out a bit more about them. Dave has been a licensee since he was 19 so knows a fair bit about the drinks industry (I'm not saying he's old, I'm saying he's a fast learner!) He's a Kendal man through and through so when he started tinkering with his own drinks Mint Cake Vodka was the obvious choice. Once that started to become successful he looked for another iconic Lake District flavour to add and came up with Gingerbread Vodka (he specifically avoided toffee vodka as he's great friends with Judith at Kin Vodka and didn't want to step on her toes). Now that has taken off he's started making fudge in collaboration with Romney's, makers of Kendal Mint Cake – I think we'll be seeing a lot more creative inventions coming from Dave over the next few years and I'm pretty sure we're going to like them all...

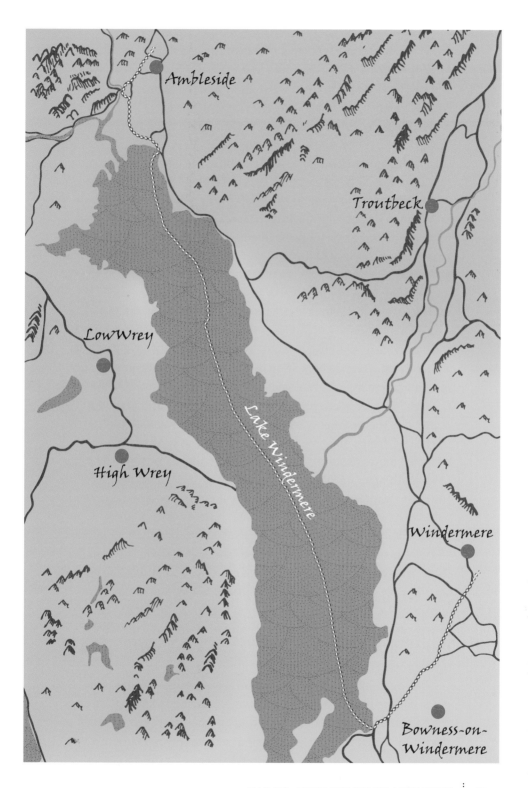

Ambleside

Troutbeck

LowWrey

Lake Windermere

High Wrey

Windermere

Bowness-on-Windermere

Today was one of our rest days. We were still heading to Ambleside but not on foot, so we poked around Bowness for a while and enjoyed a coffee in the Cornish Bakery. Well, I enjoyed a coffee while Karen polished off a pasty the size of my head. As I watched her munching away I smiled sweetly and tried not to think murderous thoughts about how she still managed to stay so wonderfully slim. I probably gained 3 pounds just sitting opposite her so I slipped out to a local shop to check out their collection of miniatures to distract myself while she finished off the final crumbs.

When we eventually reached the lake we were greeted by James from Windermere Lake Cruises, who had kindly offered us a couple of tickets to Ambleside. I first got to know James when I wrote a spoof April 1st blog which suggested that, thanks to the discovery of some underground caverns, they'd now be offering submarine tours. That was in 2016 and apparently people are still asking about them!

Due to it being slightly off season and midweek, the boat wasn't too packed, so we nabbed a couple of seats out on the upstairs deck, where Karen wrapped herself up in a couple of extra layers, dug out her flask of hot chocolate and sat back to relax and enjoy the ride, while I raced excitedly around the boat like a Haribo-fuelled 4-year-old. The weather was clearing and, as we set off up the lake, the last of the morning mist was being lit by the sun, creating a beautiful rainbow cloud around the islands ahead. I've honestly never seen anything quite like it and was really frustrated that I only had the phone with me for photos, which really didn't do it justice at all.

The cruise takes around 35 minutes so we were soon up in Ambleside. The boat docks at Waterhead Pier, roughly half a mile or so from the main town, but it's a nice easy walk, even for two people with increasingly heavy rucksacks. (Funny how a week walking with your worldly goods on your back helps you to redefine the term 'essential' – excess knickers were being jettisoned later that evening, as were the extra spare pair of 'just-in-case' trousers. I'd decided that if 'just in case' turned into reality I was quite happy to trade the lighter rucksack for soggy legs.)

The route into the town passes Ambleside Roman Fort, which dates back to the first century and was connected to Ravenglass on the west coast via Hardknott Pass, and to Brougham (just south of Penrith) via High Street fell – so called because it was once a busy

Brathay Hall

Breathtaking Brathay view of Windermere

thoroughfare and marketplace. Using an OS Map it's still relatively easy to pick out and follow the old route from Ambleside Fort all the way to Brougham, and it's a walk that's definitely on my things-to-do list.

There's evidence that the Romans grew vines in the region, though it's unlikely they produced enough grapes to make into wine. It was most likely done to remind them of home, but what we do know is that they brewed plenty of beer. To be honest, I've always felt a little bit sorry for the Roman soldiers, sent all the way from the hot climate of the Mediterranean to beautiful blustery Cumbria. It must have been quite a shock to the system, especially in the days before GORE-TEX and fluffy down jackets. Living half the year in Cyprus, I think Karen understood exactly how they felt...

After a spin around town and a spot of shopping we enjoyed the luxury of a hot coffee before heading out to find our accommodation. Given the soaking we'd got the day before and the long yomps lying ahead of us we didn't feel too guilty about a day taking it easy.

Bed for the night was at Brathay Hall and we honestly had no idea what to expect – in my mind I pictured something youth hostel-ish, but I couldn't have been further from the truth. As we walked along the huge drive towards the equally huge house set right at the head of Windermere, with spectacular views along the lake, we were both convinced that we were in the wrong place. It looked far too grand for the modest rates we were paying, so I bravely sent Karen in to reception to check things out while I took a few quick photos in case we had to make a speedy exit.

Fortunately it turned out we were in the right place and our rooms were definitely the best value for money we found on the whole trip (aside from all the lovely folks who allowed us to stay for free), plus they were also the best set up for those arriving with mucky boots. Immediately inside the door was a huge foot mat where you could remove dirty boots and soggy coats before hanging them on the adjacent coat pegs, situated over a hard floor area, allowing for easy cleaning and drip drying. Beyond that was a cabin-like room with a cosy single bed, a recessed desk and good-sized bathroom. The desk was particularly handy, as each evening we needed to write up the notes of what had happened during the day before they slipped from our minds, making writing this book a whole lot harder. (They also do luxury rooms with spectacular views if you're after something a little more cosy.)

Absolutely the only downside I could see was that it was a bit of a walk into Ambleside for dinner – not a problem in itself but the weather had chosen that evening to turn truly foul and the rain was coming down in sheets. On the bright side, we'd been invited to eat at Dodd's Restaurant, which made the walk a lot more bearable. (To be fair, there's pavement for all but 50m of the walk, you just need to remember to take a torch.)

Dodd's is a very Mediterranean restaurant, by which I mean that as well as serving some utterly delicious meals from all around the region, it has a properly Mediterranean feel to it – it's loud, bustling, a little chaotic and very laid back. They don't do reservations so you have to take your chances, but there's an excellent bar to keep you entertained and they stock the full range of Lakes Distillery gins, so you can work your way through those while you wait for a free table.

Over dinner we chatted about the sorts of things our husbands get up to while we're away – in Steve's case it's usually taking lots of photos and ploughing through all the films I'm less keen on watching. I remember my mum once saying that it was 'a good job Steve let me go on those adventures,' and it only really crossed my mind at that point that I never ask his permission. I've always been a bit of a tearaway and me taking off every now and again is just part of the deal of being married to me. I honestly couldn't imagine ever having to ask permission, or just how long he'd spend in the spare room if he tried saying 'no' – I made a mental note to appreciate that a little bit more.

Poring over the menu I realised it would be a crying shame to simply order a pizza, so I kicked off with squid before moving on to homemade gnocchi with a blue cheese sauce so divine that I never wanted it to end. As we were sitting there pondering a pudding (I honestly couldn't manage another mouthful) the waiter came over.

'The chef would like to meet you,' he said.

'What have I done?' I asked, convinced I must have used the wrong fork, or ordered the wrong combination of food, or committed some other equally heinous dining crime. Thankfully he just wanted to say hello, as we'd chatted to each other on social media for a while.

Social media gets a lot of bad press, and some of it is well deserved, but this trip would never have happened without it. As well as throwing me and Karen together, we were meeting new people and making new friends right across the county, some of whom I'll definitely be meeting up with again once the hike is done.

It was something me and Karen chatted about as we squelched home through the rain. I'm not a huge fan of the gratuitous selfie and am mortified at the idea of being recognised anywhere, but social media has the power to connect people and I love it for that. When we got back to our rooms I went to bed with a warm happy glow inside of me. Of course this glow could also have been related to the essential wine and gin tasting carried out over dinner, but wherever it came from it was nice.

Karen

Reluctantly, we locked up The Hideaway and ambled slowly down Windermere high street towards Bowness and the ferry. First, though, a quick hello to Anthony in Windermere Wines, who surprised us with a couple of bottles of Kendal Mint Cake Liqueur from Minty Mike! Glancing at the shelves I realised how many of the bottles I now recognised, and that I'd had the very good fortune to taste, just a few days into our crazy tour.

Further down the hill, a sandwich board on the pavement drew us in with the legend, 'Gin Tasting'. What actually grabbed our attention on squeezing through the door, though, was a table lined with tiny plastic shot glasses filled with amber liquid: Lakes Gingerbread Vodka.

Now I absolutely love gingerbread. Love it so much in fact that two of the places on my travel bucket list are there solely due to their links with the stuff. Nuremberg is known as the Gingerbread Capital of the World and has been baking this sweet and spicy treat for over 600 years. I've seen photos of the Nurembergers tucking into gingerbread which is way bigger than my head. Yes please. And then there's Bergen in Norway, where every year towards Christmas they make the world's biggest gingerbread city, packed with little houses, trains, cars and boats. The whole place must smell divine for weeks.

I picked up two of the little plastic glasses and combined their contents. Well, I clearly remember my science teacher at school saying that with any experiment, sample size is very important. We sampled. We sampled again. Hansel and Gretel. Christmas markets. Bonfire Night parkin. Very, very nice.

We had time to pass before our allotted ferry time over to Ambleside, so we grabbed a table in the Cornish Bakery and Beth sprang into action – updating social media, contacting producers, checking accommodation and organising visits. I scoffed a Cornish pasty.

Spotting the Peter Rabbit and Friends store as we left the cafe I was overcome with a wave of nostalgia. Nostalgia is bittersweet; it's pleasure and pain. There's supposed to be a little bit of a sense of loss, of yearning for things you can't have again, but for most people the net result is happiness. Not for me.

Seeing that little rabbit in his dinky blue jacket hits my belly like a physical blow. My children adored him; I adored their childhood. I feel so overwhelmingly sad that I can never experience that period again that I could easily cry. I would understand it if I was so dissatisfied with my life now that I just pined for better days. But that's not true at all; things are pretty good. I swallowed hard and carried on. In any case, Beth would just think the rain was causing my distress.

It's the same with smells. A whiff of Old Spice or Charlie perfume, or even the memory of Quickies face pads, can send me into a

A different (gin) slant on Windermere

tailspin. They remind me of my parents who aren't with me anymore. Heartbreak not happiness.

I know, though, that Beth is totally stumped by my indifference when she's Tigger-bouncing with excitement at the history behind some place or other. So I'd like to tell her that somewhere along the way history and nostalgia became thoroughly tangled up in my brain, with the result that I try to avoid both, albeit subconsciously. I hate nostalgia so much that I know I've tipped too far the other way. I've ended up with a weird aversion for anything that happened in the past. Sadness and tears. Ridiculous, I know, but there it is.

James from Windermere Lake Cruises met us at the ferry with tickets for our trip over the water. As we left the dock the sun was peeping through the clouds, casting intermittent bursts of light on the water. It was breezy and fresh – invigorating! In the distance a rainbow arced over the hills, dousing Ambleside in multi-coloured hues.

We docked at 1 p.m. and realised we had lots of time to kill before we could check in to our accommodation for the night. I felt a stirring of delicious anticipation.

A popular Cumbrian tourism site states: 'shopping in Cumbria isn't necessarily the first thing that may come to mind'. It isn't?

As we approached Ambleside, I spotted something which would warm the cockles of your heart, if you're anything like me: 'SALE'. But there was a compromise to be made, so first we slumped in Costa.

After a week of GORE-TEX, wicking wool, and Bridget Jones knickers (only two pairs needed, trust me), nipping in the changing rooms and squeezing into some tight white trousers and a clingy red top was exactly what I needed. Sadly, my backpack was threatening to explode at the seams so I couldn't possibly buy them, of course. But I did.

It was almost check in time. We bickered our way to Brathay Hall. A dreadful band of weather was heading in and was due to unleash itself on the area in a couple of days' time, when we faced a linear walk over the central spine of high ground between Grasmere and Keswick. Looking at the heavy rain strikes and little lightning symbols on my phone's weather app, I thought it was foolhardy to attempt it. Unless things changed. Beth was determined to do it; she would always consider the trip incomplete otherwise.

'But it's a trail we're doing,' I argued, 'not just a walk. Which means we can choose any way we like to complete the whole route. Bus, bike, car, anything!'

'I know,' Beth agreed, 'but I know what I'm like and I'll always regret it if I don't do that walk.'

'Why not do it another day, when the weather is better?'

'Hmm.'

I wasn't getting anywhere.

We stomped on along the narrow country road, dodging the showers of water thrown up by passing cars.

My irritation simmered.

'So do we have to walk back this way tonight to go to Dodd's?' I asked.

'Yep. Same way.'

'But it's chucking it down, it'll be pitch black and there's no pavement.'

'It'll be fine.'

'By taxi it will.'

We turned into the driveway to Brathay Hall. It's the home of Brathay Trust, a charity set up to improve the lives of disadvantaged young people and their families. It was all woodland and rolling fields; what a fabulous location. We rounded the stunning Georgian country house to see far-reaching views over Lake Windermere.

Our rooms were in lodges dotted around the hall. The place is just perfect for walkers, and writers too. As soon as I pushed open my room door, there was a boot-drying platform and a desk and chair, and it was cosy and warm thanks to one of those chunky radiators we all remember from school.

The rooms are compact but I can't imagine a better use of space. Everything you need is there: bed, hanging area, desk, en suite, all neatly slotted in.

We slid into our rooms, set our gear to dry, had the hottest shower we could bear, and slowly any little vexations ebbed away.

We walked the mile back into Ambleside by the light of Beth's phone.

Glance at any of a host of review sites and you'll soon get the idea that Dodd's Restaurant is rather popular. An appealing amber glow from the windows lit up the wet street as we turned the corner. It

isn't possible to book and when we arrived the place was packed, yet we waited barely 10 minutes, which gave us ample time to peruse the gins behind the bar before being ushered to our table.

I drool even now if I look at the few photos I snapped of my food that night. Goat's cheese dressed with pesto and pistachios. Swordfish and tender vegetables all glistening with tasty glazes and juices. It was the first time I'd tried baby pak choi and it won't be the last.

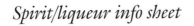

Spirit/liqueur info sheet

Product	Lakes Gingerbread Vodka
Category	21.4% ABV
Who makes it?	Mint Drinks Company. The business operates from the Punch Bowl at Barrows Green
When did it start production?	1855 according to local folklore
Where is it made?	Kendal
Key ingredients	Vodka and gingerbread [FLAVOUR, IE GINGER PLUS SUGAR?]
Where can I buy it?	http://www.mintdrinks.co.uk/mintdrinksco-cilf
*Best way to drink i*t	Great over ice or ice cream Makes a luscious liqueur coffee

A soggy, boggy yomp

By train	No train service – again, blame Wordsworth
By bus	A number of bus routes connect Ambleside to Grasmere, please check local timetables for more information
By bike	Sustrans Route 6 runs from Ambleside to Grasmere
By car	From Windermere continue along the A591 to Grasmere. There are various car parks in the village
On foot	From Brathay Hall we walked into Clappersgate then took the public footpath up over Nanny Brow onto Loughrigg. We then followed a small (soggy!) path down to the cave (marked as Quarries (dis) next to Jobson Close on OS map) before continuing on along Loughrigg Terrace and down the road into Grasmere.

Distance = 5.6 miles

The two maids of Grasmere

DAY SEVEN: Ambleside to Grasmere

Beth

As well as rather splendid rooms, Brathay Hall also offered breakfast in a light and bright cafeteria area with a good selection of breakfast goodies and plenty of room for everyone to sit. There were also magnificent views down along the lake and we lingered over breakfast perhaps a little longer than we should have. Having rested our bones yesterday, today was a fairly light and easy day; up and over Loughrigg and down into Grasmere, before my upcoming super-long hike from Grasmere to Keswick.

Back in my room, I found that packing my rucksack was now second nature and only took a few minutes. For the first few days there had been a lot of trial and error, but now everything had its place and it mostly went together like a relatively well-oiled machine. Thankfully the sun was shining, the forecast was good and we were heading over the top of a very pretty fell.

From Brathay our route took us straight up and over Nanny Brow, with stunning views all the way down and along the lake – the

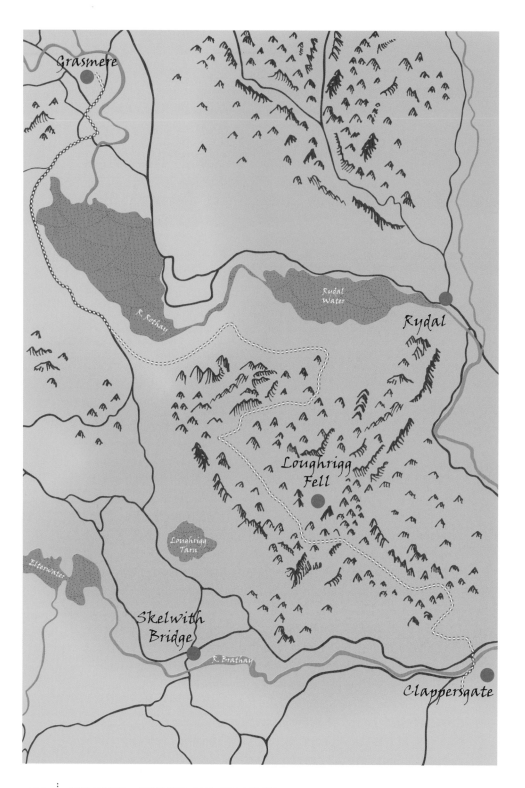

Grasmere

Rydal
Water

Rydal

R. Rothay

Loughrigg
Fell

Loughrigg
Tarn

Elterwater

Skelwith
Bridge

R. Brathay

Clappersgate

perfect excuse for me to keep pausing and catching my breath. Although Loughrigg is a very popular fell, this side of it is generally a lot quieter and we didn't see many people at all until we were closing in on the summit. One of our rest stops was next to Lily Tarn, where we met a couple with a very friendly, big, black Labrador – I knew Karen was uncomfortable around dogs and I was quite prepared to hurl myself in front of her should all the licking and tail wagging get out of hand. Luckily the pooch was far more interested in the tarn that the owners had specifically brought her to see – it turns out the dog's name was Lily and, as regular visitors to the region, they brought her here each time they came.

There are a multitude of paths criss-crossing Loughrigg and the map isn't to be entirely trusted. Routes which appear as main routes on the map often peter out into boggy nothingness, while smaller looking tracks are, in reality, main thoroughfares (I'm just lining up my excuses ready for the part where I get us a bit lost later on!). I've been up Loughrigg many times, but approaching from a different direction it took me a while to get my eye in and properly know just where I was.

The summit of Loughrigg is a special place. It is one of those small fells that punches well above its weight when it comes to the vista from the top. The beautifully clear skies affording stunning views in

Loving Loughrigg

Nanny Brow – the place, not the woman!

every direction; my favourite is to look along the valley to the iconic Langdale Pikes.

Although we weren't visiting a distillery – or off-licence – today (shockingly bad planning!) we were firmly on the stomping ground of Lanty Slee, one of the best known illicit distillers in the region. Back in the 1800s the fells were rife with illegal distillers, and stills were stashed in many a distant cave or tucked away outbuilding. One was once discovered within the walls of an old farmhouse when it was being renovated.

These illicit distillers brewed their drinks away from the eyes of the law and, like Lanty Slee (who was a farmer by day), spent the long, dark nights tending to their stills and making deliveries around the region. Many of the ingredients they needed were freely available on the fells, including the juniper, which, as well as producing the sought-after berries, also burns without much smoke and so was useful for not attracting attention.

Lanty was caught, fined and imprisoned on several occasions – often getting off perhaps a little more lightly than he should have, on account of a number of members of the judiciary being among his best customers – but as soon as he was out, he was back to his old ways. They may have found and closed down some of his stills, but they never found them all.

Heading down off the fell it's fair to say I went a little rogue with the map reading. As I said, Loughrigg has a network of different paths and, as I'm not too keen on busy routes, I was rather pleased with myself when I spotted a quiet route down off the fell, dropping towards Rydal Cave. The problem was that we were on one of those paths which fizzle out; easy to follow one minute and then disappearing into a swampy, boggy wasteland the next. Having waded through neck-high bracken for a while, and taken a couple of wrong turns, we eventually located the route down – the bad news was that it was really a bit of a quagmire after the previous day's rain, so we slipped and slithered our way down to the cave, where I promised Karen there'd be hard track all the way from there to Grasmere.

Although Rydal Caves were not, so far as I know, used by Lanty Slee I was still keen to explore all the way to the back and pretend I was a renegade brewer of illicit hooch, while Karen stayed by the entrance keeping lookout for the authorities and enjoying a rest after my botched descent. The cave is huge and has superb acoustics, and on one occasion in the past I had a thoroughly lovely time listening to a gospel choir enjoying an impromptu rehearsal.

From there the way down into Grasmere is clear, well signed and easy to follow, and we opted for the high route across Loughrigg Terrace, with its stunning views all the way up to Dunmail Raise and beyond. The gentle walk along the road into the village was the perfect way to stretch out our legs without having to rush too much. As we wound through the streets we passed the tiny but globally renowned Gingerbread Shop (which we thought about going into but decided against on account of our enormous backpacks and the huge crowd of people already queuing outside), and St Oswald's Church, where William Wordsworth and members of his family are buried.

Nanny Brow woodland

We couldn't pass by the Herdy shop, though, as my good friends there had arranged for us to pick up a couple of Herdy mugs to cheer us on our journey – now we had proper china mugs for our morning tea to go with our beautiful Cumbria Crystal glasses, which were still remarkably unscathed in our rucksacks. I'm not sure if there's a world record for hiking the farthest whilst carrying a rucksack full of fragile items, but if there is I'm pretty sure we could claim it. Stinky socks and mildly whiffy t-shirts were deployed to keep everything safe and secure and we seemed to be doing okay so far.

Our hostel was just outside the village, though thankfully near enough to nip back into to get food. As we checked in we noticed they had a lot of food and drink on sale in the reception area, and they told us that the kitchens were superbly equipped.

'So long as they've got a corkscrew we'll be happy,' we joked.

'Only alcohol sold on the premises is allowed to be drunk here,' they replied, 'you haven't brought any alcohol in with you have you?'.

Me and Karen looked at each other. By this stage of the journey our rucksacks were better stocked than your average Oddbins, but our Gin Sherpa was due later and we had no intention of risking the confiscation all of our goodies.

'No,' we said innocently, both deploying the sort of nervous smile you use when sauntering through the 'Nothing to Declare' channel on your way back from hols, knowing full well there's a bottle of exotic spirit stashed at the bottom of your suitcase – the sort of thing which tasted beautiful in the sunshine but back in Blighty has a faint whiff of cough syrup about it. Now I knew how Lanty Slee must have felt.

We gently walked up the stairs, praying that nothing would clink and give us away, and quickly found our room. Karen kindly let me bag the bottom bunk so I could get a good night's sleep, as we'd already decided we'd be going our separate ways in the morning – only for the day though. The weather report was dire, so we'd decided to split up; Karen was to take the bus from Grasmere to Keswick, while I was going to don every waterproof I had and tackle the walk. In answer to the question you're probably asking yourself right now, yes, I'd clearly taken leave of my senses.

In preparation for my epic hike I'd also summoned Steve the Gin Sherpa for one final visit – if I was going to be hiking 13 miles in the pouring rain I really didn't want to be carrying any more than I absolutely had to. Me and Karen pooled our collective items to go into one bag and were both amazed at how heavy it felt in our hands – when you carry something in your hands you know immediately when it's heavy as it's annoying from the start, but when it's strapped to your back in a rucksack you don't notice it so quickly, though it does tend to wear you down over the course of the day.

Steve merrily whisked away all our excess items, and I'd really like to tell you that my rucksack felt as light as a feather now, but it honestly didn't and I was definitely getting a little concerned about the following day's hike. I'd walked that distance many times before, and I'd walked in foul conditions too, but to set out on my own, knowing that I was going to get soaked to the skin and not have Steve around to bicker about the route with, was a little daunting.

I'd taken every sensible precaution I could think of: triple checked the weather (I'd seen thunder forecast but not until much later in the day, by which time I planned to be safely in the B&B), triple checked the route, triple checked my wet weather gear, logged the route on a shared app so Steve knew exactly where I'd be, and promised I'd text at regular intervals so he could track my journey. But I was still unsettled. I decided I needed a nice relaxing evening, so I did the most sensible thing I could think of: I downed an enormous chilli, accompanied by a couple of large glasses of red wine, topped it off with a nightcap from my gin stash, and got a nice early night. When I returned to our room Karen was in the top bunk making her notes from the day, and probably preparing a shopping list or two

Rydal Water – look out for the caves

for her relaxing day exploring Grasmere and Keswick, while I drifted off to sleep in the bottom bunk, dreaming of waterfalls and giant wellington boots.

Karen

Breakfast at Brathay was a real feast. A full English, fruits, yoghurts, muffins, toast and all laid out buffet style so we made sure to fill our boots ready to fuel us up Loughrigg later that morning.

As we set off to find the start of the day's hike, Beth made her usual post breakfast comment: 'It'll be all uphill for a bit.'

Beth's 'bit' is a variable beast and today it was around two hours.

We headed towards the summit of Loughrigg, hugging a stone wall to keep us on track. In usual Lakeland fashion there was lots of up, some fell walking, lots of down and, today, a couple of tarns.

'You'll need talcum powder for that.'

By now, I was used to folk pitching in with advice on Squeaky the Backpack. Most days we hadn't seen anyone for miles, so squeaky went unchallenged, but it was Saturday and with the sun forcing a peep around the clouds today, Loughrigg was awash with walkers.

Beth mingled with the crowds at the trig point whilst just below I wedged myself against a rock and snuck a coffee and chunk of cake.

We prepared to head down towards Grasmere. Everyone was snaking down a well-travelled path from the summit so, naturally, Beth decided we couldn't possibly follow suit. We had to be adventurous. Explorers.

After consulting the map on her phone, she headed off towards the bogs. We squelched through waist-high prickly stuff, knee-deep gunk and goo for miles. Beth was on a mission to ensure that not a single day passed when my feet stayed dry; last night's attempt at waterproofing my boots was no match. I had to keep stopping to check, am I walking *by* the stream or *in* the stream? Finally we skidded down to Rydal Cave and I stuffed in eight jelly babies for comfort.

So, on to Grasmere via a path cluttered with *so many people*. One great thing about the recent appalling weather was that we'd had the paths and tracks pretty much to ourselves. Today, my face ached from all those 'Hi's!'

'You'll need Vaseline for that.' Squeaky was playing up again.

Beth's head was full of woolly sheep as she set her sights on the Herdy shop. I was focused acutely on my bladder. There were too many people around for my usual 'anywhere will do' approach to peeing. I took a deep breath and squeezed all relevant muscles.

'Not far,' Beth assured me. 'We're heading down into Grasmere now.'

Which was all well and good but I couldn't help noticing that we were still climbing. Finally, I spotted the queue snaking out of the Gingerbread Shop and I knew we'd arrived.

As Beth was about to be sucked into the Herdy shop I threw my backpack at her and raced down the road for the little girl's room. At bursting point, I sprinted into the building, whereupon my legs slammed into a turnstile.

I stopped, panting, and considered my options: my coins were in my backpack. Just then two girls came out of the cubicles and as they made for the exit the barrier opened. Here was my chance.

As they came through and passed by me, I flung myself forwards just as the jaws of the thing snapped shut on my right thigh. The rest of me had made it through, though, so after a thorough bout of wrestling I was a free woman again and could complete my mission.

To all who would tut and shake their heads at my blatantly bucking the system, I would like to point out in my defence that installing a coin-operated barrier between a loo and a full bladder is just asking for trouble.

I limped back and binge-cuddled a Herdy.

We checked into YHA Grasmere, where we tossed a coin for the bottom bunk and I lost.

Beth went off to slurp coffee and write blogs so I left her in peace. I was feeling a lot better about her proposed high fell, bad weather hike to Keswick the next day. I'd felt so guilty – how could I let her go off on her own? We were in this together. But my instincts screamed 'NO'! The weather forecast was foul; thick mist, heavy, persistent rain all day and a chance of thunderstorms.

But Beth was much more familiar with the fells than me. I hike as often as I can but she hikes more. On the other hand, I've hiked solo more than she has. And often in places where I took bear spray or anti-venom with me. What I'm trying to say is that neither of us is reckless and we have great respect for the outdoors and Mother Nature. Even though we disagreed completely on the best way to get to Keswick under the circumstances, I felt fairly confident that if Beth felt up to the hike then she would pull it off without incident.

So, we'd come to an agreement. Beth had set up a system whereby her husband, Steve, could track her as she went. All three of us knew her exact route. And I would be going to Keswick by bus.

As I did every evening, I scribbled down some notes while everything was all fresh in my mind.

Before I came up to Cumbria, one of my daughters had filled me in on the new gin craze in the UK, but it was still a surprise to actually see folk putting their heads together and coming up with all these delicious new combinations. Everyone is looking for a unique twist and there seems to be a gin for everyone. It's not like it used to be, when you'd head into a bar and just ask for a gin and tonic; now, you're likely to be handed an extensive tasting menu, complete with tonic water and garnish recommendations. It's not just gin either. There are new vodkas, whiskies, rums, brandies and liqueurs springing up all over the country.

It was time to sooth my aching muscles. I toddled off down the corridor in search of the shower block. The shower was wonderfully powerful and piping hot and the cubicle was huge; plenty of room to stretch out and dry off properly, which sadly I couldn't make the most of with my postage stamp-sized microfibre towel. Admittedly, these towels are just fabulous for multi-day backpacking. They're incredibly light to carry, pack up into a tiny square and soak up lots of water. It's just that I feel like I'm rubbing myself with a chamois leather and it really sets my teeth on edge. It's the chalk screech on the blackboard at school, the squeal of polystyrene, the squeak of a cotton wool ball.

Mind you, some of the things that give us the jitters are just plain odd. Did you know there's a Facebook support group for Anatidaephobia? Anatidaephobia is the irrational fear that somehow, somewhere, you are being watched by a duck. I also once knew someone who would almost go into meltdown if a wooden chip shop fork touched their teeth. And someone else who was seriously freaked out by soggy beer mats. Good job Beth and I are not affected; so far the trip has been full of both of those.

Spirit/liqueur info sheet

THEN

Product	Moonshine. This name was generally applied to any high proof spirit that was made illegally
Who made it?	Moonshiners! Moonshining started in Britain and the name comes from the fact that to avoid getting caught the moonshiners made their illicit alcohol in the dark of night
What was it?	Moonshine was strong alcohol and packed quite a punch. It was a risky business for both moonshiners and their customers. The biggest problem was that it was made undercover so there weren't any guidelines or regulations imposed to make sure that it was safe to drink
What was it made of?	Made from grain, white sugar, fruit in rather unsanitary conditions
When did it start production?	16th/17th-century Britain
Why? What inspired it?	The whole point of making moonshine was to avoid laws, taxes and regulations. Folk in many countries have dabbled in their own illegal alcohol production. The Irish have their Poitín (pronounced 'potcheen,') with its shockingly high alcohol strength of up to 90%! No wonder the Irish word for hangover is póit or póite
Where was it made?	In secret!

NOW

Is it still illegal?	With strict regulation, licence requirements and tax obligations, moonshine has become legalised in various countries over the last few years. The name has stayed but the quality is controlled
What is it made of?	Grain, sugar, yeast, and water

Going our separate ways

By train	No train service
By bus	A number of bus routes connect Grasmere to Keswick, please check local timetables for more information
By bike	Sustrans Route 6 runs from Wythburn to Keswick
By car	From Grasmere continue along the A591 to Keswick. There are various car parks in the town
On foot	From Grasmere I headed up the A591 to Wythburn then around Thirlmere to Dob Gill. I then followed the public footpath alongside Dob Gill to Harrop tarn and on to Blea Tarn. I remained on the path down into Watendlath then followed the road down to Derwent Water and picked up the lakeside path into town

Distance = 13 miles

Dob Gill and still smiling

DAY EIGHT:
Grasmere to Keswick

Beth

Today didn't so much dawn as bubble to the surface. I'd paid a little extra for the full breakfast to set me up for my day and, having woken up before my alarm went off, I crept out quietly and left Karen snoozing in bed. At least I thought I'd left her snoozing; what I hadn't realised was that although I'd woken up before my alarm I'd actually forgotten to switch it off, so a few minutes after I left the room it went off waking up Karen. As if that wasn't bad enough, in my desire to crack on I'd already packed the alarm deep in my rucksack so Karen could hear it, she couldn't find it. She was terribly nice about it when I finally reappeared but I can only imagine the names she must have been calling me at the time (I know the names *I* would have been calling me if I had been Karen right then!).

Breakfast had been a delightfully huge fry-up; I'd gone for the full works, including runny-yolked eggs. Karen has a real thing about eggs and although she'd insisted that I should carry on and have them regardless, I'd avoided them out of politeness – I have a real

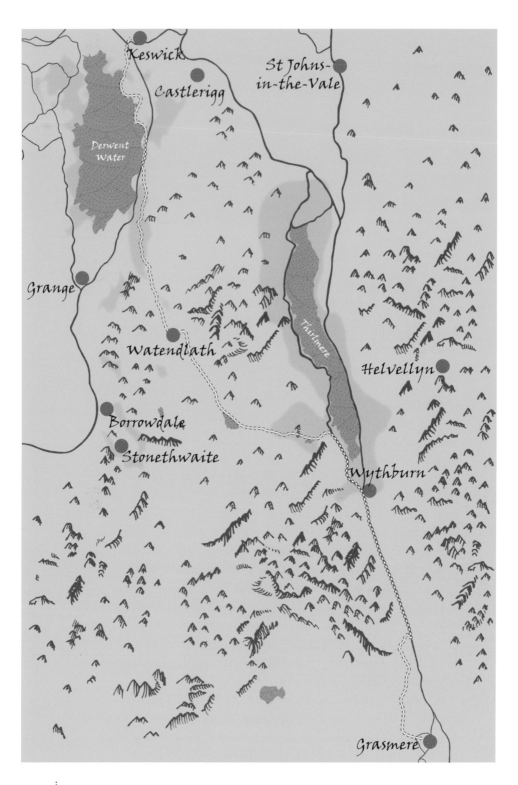

Keswick

Castlerigg

St Johns-in-the-Vale

Derwent Water

Grange

Watendlath

Thirlmere

Helvellyn

Borrowdale

Stonethwaite

Wythburn

Grasmere

thing about dentists and I wouldn't want someone having root canal treatment while I was trying to eat my toast. Anyway, I'd been perfectly content with my regular order of a bacon sarnie with grilled tomatoes which each and every establishment had been more than happy to make for me. (Have you ever noticed how, despite the bacon sandwich being a staple of the British breakfast table it's so rarely offered at hotels? I even had a hotel in London refuse to make me one – they agreed to serve me bread, bacon and tomatoes on a plate, but refused to assemble them into sandwich form. Honestly!)

Full to the gills and itching to get going I collected my rucksack from our room, bid Karen farewell and headed off. I was glad to be getting a good early start. The rain had eased for a little while, although the guy I passed in the car park on my way out still gave me an odd look as I waved a cheery good morning to him. My first mission was to 'put my foot down' along the road section to keep myself well ahead and get up Dunmail Raise to the foot of Dob Gill, and I was pretty pleased to make it in just over an hour and a quarter.

It was such a shame the weather was against us and we didn't have the leeway to wait for a better day, as our original plan had been to spend the first part of the journey paying homage to Benjamin, the central character of Wordsworth's poem 'The Waggoner,' and visiting a number of the hostelries along the way. The Waggoner charts the journey of Benjamin as he drives his coach and horses up and over

The delightful Ashness Bridge, one of the most photographed in the Lake District

Dunmail Raise during a pretty grim night – the route from Grasmere to Keswick was one of the last coaching routes in the country on account of the fact that Wordsworth and friends successfully blocked the building of a railway through the area, so coach and horses plugged the gap before cars came along. Whether you're walking or driving keep your eyes peeled for the many drinking troughs along the way, which would have kept the horses going on the long uphill haul – there's a lovely one right next to the Grasmere roundabout.

Up at Dob Gill I took a few long gulps of coffee, stuffed a couple of slabs of chocolate in my mouth and began heading upwards. The ground was sodden and, with the rain now falling steadily, the path was more like a stream for most of the way up, making it less like hiking and more like ghyll scrambling. Harrop Tarn was a lovely surprise at the top, as was the broad, hard track leading away into the woods – I'd definitely been expecting something a little less well defined.

Winding my way through the woods I bumped into a man in a flat cap with two whippets and was momentarily concerned that the rain was causing me to hallucinate northern clichés. I think we all surprised each other a bit in the middle of this remote woodland in the pouring rain. Some people have asked if I'm scared of walking alone in case I bump into someone whose intentions are less than honourable. To be honest I'm cautious rather than scared, and I'm more wary of the environment than the people I might meet in it – if someone wants to prey on the vulnerable I can't imagine they're going to hang around the top of a sodden, windy fell on the off chance of finding someone to pick on. We nodded our hellos, exchanged traditional British comments about the weather, and continued our separate ways.

Things definitely got more interesting once I was out of the woods, and the route alongside Blea Tarn had a consistency somewhere between oxtail soup and Marmite – it's a place I can't imagine drying out all that often, although I was treated to the sight of a beautiful rainbow as I paused to add a layer of clothing. I may have been tired but the only time on the entire hike that my spirits dropped was when I couldn't locate the gate leading down to Watendlath, so I started singing 'Watendlath' to the tune of 'Here we go' to keep myself going. It's the little things.

Harrop Tarn, 'a lovely surprise at the top'

Dropping down to Watendlath I slipped and fell a few times, and the third time I went down I decided to stay down and sledge the hill on my backside to save a few bruises. I knew there was a National Trust cafe at Watendlath and held out a very vague hope that it may be open. But no, all I found was a disconsolate fisherman sheltering under the eaves of a nearby barn quietly muttering oaths to himself.

There's a good public footpath from Watendlath down to Derwent Water, but by now I was utterly soaked to the skin and getting cold – no disrespect to my waterproofs at all but the rain and wind had barely let up for a minute, so I decided to take the easier option and stick to the road. On my way down I paused for coffee and painkillers. Two men passed me as I slumped against the wall; they were heading up and although they appeared to have decent boots on their 'waterproofs' were the light ponchos you find at a theme park. I tried to warn them what the conditions were like but they insisted they were going to make it to the Langdales – several miles and numerous hills away. I've no idea whether they did or not, but wherever they ended up they would have been soaked.

The route down is blessed with two of the best views in the county (so long as it isn't pouring down): Surprise View and Ashness Bridge. Most of the times when you visit there are other plenty of other people around and it can be tricky taking a nice clean photograph without any other humans in it, but I didn't have that problem today – can't imagine why! With the sun now making a very occasional foray through the clouds I was treated to rainbows at both locations, so there was still plenty to smile about as I squelched my way towards Keswick.

My early start meant I made it into Keswick by 2 p.m. I was a bit early for checking in to the B&B and I wasn't too sure where Karen was, plus I was exhausted and in need of a friendly face, so I popped in to see my good friends Alex and Kerrie at Keswick Boot Company to tell them how the boots they'd sold me had stood up to the hike so far. Alex took one look at me, sat me down, told me to mind the shop and ran out to buy me a huge coffee. I'm honestly not sure what I would have done if a proper customer had come in – by that stage I may have been able to mutter the word 'boots' and gesticulate vaguely towards the wall of assorted footwear. As I looked around at all the boots that surrounded me the only thing I could think of was how dry they looked and how cosy my feet would have felt in them right at that moment – my AKUs had done a sterling job but I would have required a pair of waders and a wetsuit to escape today's weather intact. I also picked up some lovely gifts left there for us by the Twig Pen People – a set of beautifully engraved Twig Pens and keyrings to remember our journey.

Tearing myself away from the nice warm shop I headed off in search of the B&B, pausing along the way for supplies (Alex politely didn't tell me until later that I'd left a huge wet bum print on the bench in his shop). Karen was already there and was glad to see I'd made it in one piece and surprised that I'd heard none of the thunder that she had noticed. I managed to mumble a few things about

my journey before closing the door, removing every sodden item of clothing, having a very long, hot shower, and polishing off most of a small bottle of Lakes Distillery Damson Gin which counted as a) one of my five a day, b) an essential herbal remedy for my cold bones, and c) research ahead of our trip there in a couple of days time.

Finally returning to feeling something like human I was now ravenously hungry, so I grabbed Karen and headed for The George and their legendary pies. Although this entire trip has revolved around gin and assorted other spirits, this was another of those 'I need a pint, a pie and some chips' nights. As we chatted and laughed and compared notes about our very different days – Karen's appeared to be a lot drier and contained a lot more cake – we demolished our enormous plate of food.

The only ill effects I was feeling was a sore hip from my falls near Watendlath and a blister on one of my toes. I was, however, spectacularly tired, so we headed back early and I immediately collapsed into bed. There's something quite wonderful about doing a long, challenging hike then crawling into a clean, warm bed with a full stomach and aching limbs; a feeling I appreciated fully for around 30 seconds before I fell fast asleep.

Karen

Beth set off early to face her 13-mile hike in the pouring rain.

'Best of luck! See you in Keswick.'

I turned over in my bunk and snoozed a while before packing up and heading off in search of a bus to Keswick.

A vast blanket of grey hung heavy over the hills. As far as my eye could see, everything was stony grey; the houses, the pavements, the hills. Thunder rumbled continuously in the background.

I sheltered in the bus stop; I'd only walked the ten minutes from the hostel and was already drenched. I hoped Beth was faring well in the hills.

Several hikers joined me in the shelter, having abandoned their plans for the day; Keswick pubs and coffee shops were going to have a field day. We all piled onto the bus, backpacks squeezed into every available space. From the comfort of the bus I had hoped to take in the views, but the hills were almost shrouded by now and the rain was coming down in a thick pelt and streaming down the windows. There was a sudden giant peal of thunder which I swear could be felt through the bus seat.

Dig the twig!

My first goal was to get rid of my backpack to make way for the day I had in mind. I successfully offloaded it at my first point of call, that evening's B&B. I was now really looking forward to a potter around Keswick. Beth hates shopping and she'd already suffered in Ambleside. In any case it really is best if I'm on my own if shopping is involved. I like to dip in and out of shops when the fancy takes me or whenever something catches my eye. In fact, in abject despair my husband once secretly recorded my movements when he was following me around the shops, and the resultant trace was more tangled than a bowl of upturned spaghetti. The one and only time my husband has ever been desperate to get into a clothes shop was in Auckland. It was Topshop and he was incensed as he'd spotted a tie online that he wanted to wear to a wedding, but the store had closed its doors while Madonna did a bit of private browsing.

A quick glance at the faces of today's shoppers and I'd say to Keswick town planners: get yourself a man crèche. I first spotted one of these at the Trafford Centre in Manchester. I think they were trialling it at the time but how could it not be a success? Basically, it's somewhere to drop your chap off while you go shopping, the fellas being easily lured in with a PlayStation controller.

The Germans called it a Männergarten (which literally translates as 'men's garden') and when Ikea decided to jump on the bandwagon they opened Manland in Sydney. There's all sorts of fun stuff in there, from model railways, TV sport, magazines and the like. To add to the fun, there's sometimes a wristband system just to make sure that the chaps are picked up by the right person at the end of the day. The shopping partner also receives buzzer reminders to ensure the men are actually collected at all.

And far from taking umbrage, any chaps I've spoken to have been quite taken with the concept. Take my husband. At the time he was a 747 pilot, yet he was totally unfazed by the idea of being treated like a naughty toddler being dropped at preschool. He was ridiculously excited at the prospect, only turning to ask, 'You will come back and pick me up, won't you?'

The rain was torrential but there were steamy shop windows displaying huge slabs of cake, pubs with inviting interiors and *all those shops*. And finally unencumbered by my backpack, I could safely go in. And there's a rule, of course, that however full your backpack, there's always room for new clothes. A new pouch opens up. It's a bit like everyone knowing that you can eat food from Marks and Spencer until your heart's content as it has no calories.

I immediately fell in love with a 'light as a feather' insulated jacket. I badly wanted this but obviously it's not much use in Cyprus. I'll have to move.

And then, unbelievably, I found that my credit card was actually *hot*; I kid you not, it was warm to the touch. Is it possible that your husband can set it to self-combust? Burrowing into my pocket where the card had been I realised that I'd somehow activated a gel hand warmer in there.

Then to my delight, I spotted a wishing well.

I remember when I was a little girl, we used to go to a pub with a wishing well. We'd go there, my parents, my brother and I, and my dad would plonk his pint of bitter on a table outside with a sigh of happiness and we'd clamber around his legs, mithering for coins to throw into the well.

It was such an important job, getting it right. It had to be the right wish, the coin had to be thrown *just so* and at *exactly* the right moment when your eyes were still squeezed tight.

I still can't resist it. And of course you must never tell anyone what you've wished for...

I opened my eyes just as my coin was in its final spiral down the funnel before it disappeared. There. It was done.

Making my way back to the B&B, I was irresistibly drawn towards the warming, amber lights of a bar. I sheltered under its canopy, desperately searching for a reason to go in there. There was one, I just knew it. And then it came to me. Beth and I had already had a little taster of Bedrock Gin on our very first day of the trip in the fabulous gin parlour at Virginia House. I'd had a couple of glasses of wine just before that though, so I didn't feel I'd really done it justice. A resampling was necessary.

As happens so often, it was a chance conversation in a pub that inspired Vince Wilkins to launch his company, Spirit of the Lakes. It was back in 2008 but he already had an inkling that gin was going to soar in popularity over the next few years. Vince got together with a distillery in the Midlands and the result was Bedrock Gin, made using the beautifully clear spring water from Ennerdale glacial lake and with a rather interesting addition of oak bark sourced from a sawmill near Bassenthwaite.

The gin is made with 13 botanicals, including juniper, coriander seeds, angelica root, lemon peel, orange peel, cassia, liquorice, nutmeg and cinnamon, and the oak bark. I'd slowly come to realise that, in gin making, angelica is often regarded as the third major ingredient after juniper and coriander seeds. I'd also learnt a bit about cassia, which tastes like cinnamon only stronger. Bakers often use it and if you've had cinnamon buns or muffins, then you've probably had cassia.

We'd come across some really creatively named spirits on this trip and if the name 'Bedrock' conjures up solid images of the Lakeland landscape for you, then that's just as the makers intended.

For once, as I wasn't carrying my home on my back and I wasn't caked head to toe in mud and cow dung, I couldn't possibly miss the opportunity of nipping into that bar and, in the name of research, ordering a Bedrock. Neat, for starters.

As a gin lover, it really is fun to learn how to taste gin properly. So, if you're reading this book and in a position to play along, I'll wait while you tip a little gin into your glass. You'll need a little jug of water too.

Remember to start off neat; no ice, no tonic, no garnish. If you slosh in the tonic right away it will mask some of the botanical flavours, and for a novice, it makes it more difficult to pick out the botanicals.

Now, give your gin a quick swirl to release the aromas before easing your nose into the glass for a gentle sniff. What can you smell? As a clue, the most common aromas are citrus, fruit, floral, earthy and spicy.

My glass of Bedrock is giving out definite hints of juniper and something floral too.

If you're struggling you can reduce the alcohol blast a little and get a much better sense of the aromas by placing your hand over the top of your glass to cover it and then briefly tipping it over just enough to wet your palm with the gin. Then, wipe your hands without rubbing, cup them together, pop your nose in and sniff.

I would join in but I'm in a bar, the décor is terribly smart and I don't want to alarm the staff.

Now you're ready to taste. Take a sip. If you really want to go pro you can slurp, and I would myself if only Beth was here and I could just pretend it was her.

Swirl it around your mouth. What can you taste? Pine? Citrus? You'll inevitably sense warmth in your mouth and a kick at the back of the throat. It's early days for me in my tasting prowess, but in the last week or so I've certainly picked out liquorice, citrus and a few floral hints. Juniper is *piney*.

My Bedrock tastes of juniper, citrus, possibly coriander, and was that liquorice?

Don't worry if it doesn't come easily. Try pouring a few drops of water into your gin and diluting the alcohol a little; you may then find that some of the botanicals are easier to detect. I haven't mastered this bit yet, but I'm working on it.

It was almost dark outside and I felt I ought to head off to the B&B, but to be honest it had been dark for pretty much the entire day, so for the sake of completeness, I opted to try some Bedrock with added tonic and garnish first.

Spent and happy, I returned to the B&B. Lounging on the bed, I held my breath as the doorbell rang downstairs. *I hope it's Beth.*

Then her familiar voice drifted up the stairs as she – I imagined

– was pulling off her boots and stowing her stick. I heard the weary tread of her feet ascending the stairs and proffered a tub of strawberries and a mountain of cake through her room door.

'How did it go?'

It's fair to say that everything was soaked. She was exhausted and she'd had a couple of falls, slicing through her trousers, but *she was back and she was fine.*

And she carried good news: she'd had a tip-off from Alex from Keswick Boot Company who said that the George Hotel made the most incredible pies.

'Beware of the big one!' he'd implored. 'You'll see what I mean.'

We went.

'For those people with a BIG appetite, why not try one of our famous homemade George Gigantic Pies'.

Unfortunately, I'd eaten a giant baguette just before Beth's pie announcement and when I saw the size of even the half portion of pie, I knew I couldn't manage it. The gods were looking down on me, though, as Beth faded halfway through eating hers, nearly face-planting the table. Well, it would have been downright bad manners to send back such an iconic pie only half eaten...

Sometimes only pie will do

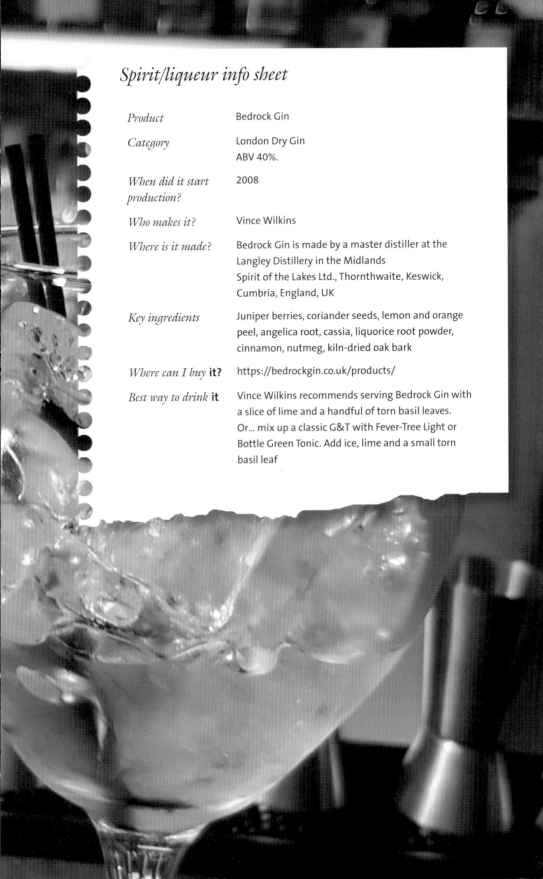

Spirit/liqueur info sheet

Product	Bedrock Gin
Category	London Dry Gin ABV 40%.
When did it start production?	2008
Who makes it?	Vince Wilkins
Where is it made?	Bedrock Gin is made by a master distiller at the Langley Distillery in the Midlands Spirit of the Lakes Ltd., Thornthwaite, Keswick, Cumbria, England, UK
Key ingredients	Juniper berries, coriander seeds, lemon and orange peel, angelica root, cassia, liquorice root powder, cinnamon, nutmeg, kiln-dried oak bark
Where can I buy **it?**	https://bedrockgin.co.uk/products/
Best way to drink **it**	Vince Wilkins recommends serving Bedrock Gin with a slice of lime and a handful of torn basil leaves. Or... mix up a classic G&T with Fever-Tree Light or Bottle Green Tonic. Add ice, lime and a small torn basil leaf

Twizy time!

By train	No train service
By bus	A number of bus routes connect Keswick to Armathwaite Hall; please check local timetables for more information
By bike	Sustrans Route 38 runs along Bassenthwaite from Keswick – you'll just need a short detour from the route to reach Armathwaite Hall/ Lakes Distillery
By car	From Keswick take the A66 alongside Bassenthwaite (watch for the average speed limit cameras). At the end of the lake follow the B5291 to Lakes Distillery/ Armathwaite Hall
On Foot	Follow the public footpath from Keswick to Derwent Bridge and then on to High Stock Bridge. Turn left to follow the A591 briefly then pick up the parallel track at Dancing Gate. When you rejoin the A591 turn left to find the footpath leading through Mirehouse and eventually alongside the lake, emerging at Cottage Wood, next to Armathwaite Hall.

Distance = 7.5 miles

DAY NINE: Keswick to Armathwaite Hall

Beth

We'd explained our journey to lots of people along the way but I don't recall anyone looking at us quite as oddly as the landlord at that B&B. The place was beautiful and the food fabulous, but he clearly couldn't figure us out at all, and he had the sort of polite 'okaaaay' look on his face that you might use when a previously well-respected family member announces that they genuinely believe the earth is flat. The breakfast was great though, so I wasn't arguing.

Today was mostly another rest day, which I was very glad of. I'd tried to describe to Karen what we were doing, but there's no way of saying 'we're going to be driving around Cumbria in an electric sheep' which doesn't elicit exactly the same sort of response we'd seen from the landlord earlier. The electric sheep are Renault Twizys, small electric cars with big personalities. They can be found right across the county but the 10 in Cumbria have all been painted as sheep and are named in honour of the old Cumbrian dialect, still used by some farmers, for sheep counting: Yan, Tyan, Tethera,

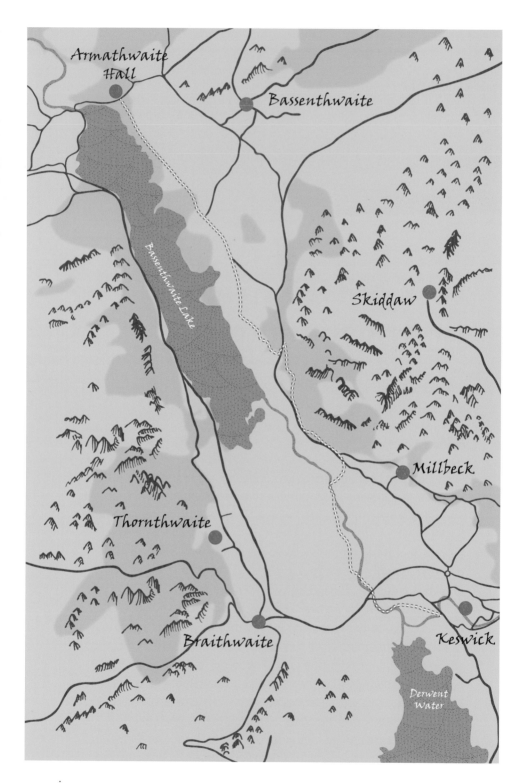

Armathwaite
Hall

Bassenthwaite

Bassenthwaite Lake

Skiddaw

Millbeck

Thornthwaite

Braithwaite

Keswick

Derwent
Water

Methera, Pip, Sethera, Lethera, Hovera, Dovera and Dec.

Our particular 'sheep' for the day was Thethera, which lives at the Keswick Brewing Company. We'd planned a brewery tour for the afternoon but the morning was to be spent zooming around Bassenthwaite visiting the homes of Langtons and Bedrock gins. As we arrived at the brewery Karen squeaked with delight at the sight of our chariot – whatever you may have been expecting it's unlikely to match the fabulous reality of a sheep-shaped car.

The owners of the brewery, Nigel and Sue, gave us a quick rundown on the controls and let us stash our rucksacks in their storeroom – the Twizy may be fab but it's not got a lot of luggage space. As I'm lucky enough to be able to pop back up for a spin whenever I fancy, I let Karen take charge of the driving and I literally took a back seat and acted as navigator (you sit one behind the other in a Twizy). There was much giggling and laughter as we edged out into Keswick traffic.

At this point I should mention that the Twizy has 2 horns, one normal level car horn and one comedic small horn for warning pedestrians of your approach – being electric it's easy to sneak up on people in a Twizy. I expect James Bond could make good use of one on his next adventure; the last thing Blofeld would suspect is Bond creeping up on him in an electric sheep. I think it's fair to say that Karen took rather a shine to the pedestrian horn and took to beeping it any time we saw anyone, regardless of whether they were about to step in front of us or not – we made a lot of people smile as we drove by beeping and waving.

Our first stop was on the north side of the lake at the foot of Skiddaw, home to Langtons gin. Although we'd not been able to meet up I'd had a chat to Langtons' owner, Nick Dymoke-Marr, who'd filled me in a little on how their gin is made. They get all their water from an aquifer 330ft beneath Skiddaw, which is accessed via a little cabin in the woods somewhere behind the Lyzzick Hall hotel (who obviously stock a fine range of Langtons gins).

The water is pumped up from there and taken away for distillation to Nick's exceptionally high standards. The gin produced is very light and delicate and a lot less 'ginny' than many others. Nick's uncompromising approach to his work means that everything from the bottles to the gin are of consistently high quality. Langtons is a big gin for a global market and can be found in bars and fine food stockists such as Selfridges and Harvey Nichols.

Continuing around the lake we decided to stop at the Lakes Distillery for tea and cake — we'd be back here for the full tour tomorrow, but the weather was so nice that we thought we'd get some photos in today (and if that isn't a convincing enough excuse for a cake stop then I don't know what is!). We also checked out our accommodation for the night at Armathwaite Hall, where

Motorised sheep!?

Karen zoomed up the driveway a little over enthusiastically, didn't spot a speed hump and nearly put me through the roof.

The Twizy has a range of 30 to 40 miles, depending on the terrain you're covering. Recharging points are dotted around the county, though no special connectors are needed so anywhere with a normal 3-pin plug will do (you might want to ask if they mind first though; charging your phone is one thing but plugging your car in could attract attention!). If you borrow the one from Keswick Brewing Company you can make it all the way over to Honister Slate Mine, where they'll be happy to recharge your car ready for the return journey while you enjoy a tour and a spot of lunch.

Heading back along the south side of the

lake we passed through Thornthwaite, which is home to Bedrock Gin. Of all the producers, these were the only people we never managed to speak with, despite many attempts via email and phone – there's a fine line between persistence and stalking and I was worried that I may be crossing it. We'd sampled Bedrock gin back at the beginning of our hike in Virginia House and I was pretty sure there'd be more Bedrock before our journey was over – especially as Karen was at least one Bedrock ahead of me after her cheeky tasting session when I was getting soaked on the fells.

Not wanting to miss a photo op I directed Karen up through Whinlatter Forest to a lovely layby that has perfect views across Bassenthwaite Lake to Skiddaw. We passed a couple of cyclists on the way up and one of them pulled in to chat to us about the car as we admired the view, proving that you're never alone in a Twizy.

We made it back to the brewery in one piece, and in her eagerness to get to the beer Karen even took a shortcut the wrong way along a one way street (just don't tell anyone else and we'll be fine).

Keswick Brewing Company started in 2006 but there's been a brewery on this site as far back as 1855, possibly earlier, and they have an impressive collection of many of the old bottles. Beer has the same 4 basic ingredients – grain, water, hops and yeast – but it's amazing how many different flavours those four things can produce. As well as their four staple beers – Keswick Gold, Bitter, Thirst Quencher and Keswick Special Bitter – they create an impressive array of seasonal brews and charity ales, as well as a beer advent calendar.

They are also very generous with the samples at the end of tour and, with Karen reliving her student days and pulling pints behind the bar, we were soon a very merry band of visitors indeed, swapping stories and getting to know each other.

Sadly, all good tours must come to an end, so we bid farewell to Nigel, Sue and all our new best mates and headed for the bus station. Due to roadworks along the north of the lake the bus dropped us on the A66, with both the driver and assorted passengers offering us directions to Armathwaite Hall – it was only a mile or so up the road but the walk helped to clear some of the beer from my system.

Armathwaite Hall is stunningly luxurious and easily the poshest place we stayed on the trek, but they're still friendly enough to welcome you with big backpacks and muddy boots. I'll admit that beautiful and friendly though it was, I'm still slightly intimidated by such places – I've never stayed in posh hotels and am always worried that I'm doing, saying or ordering the wrong thing. Leaving Karen to soak in a hot bath, I disappeared off down to the cosy lounge area for a spot of reading. The barman asked if I wanted a drink and I meant to say 'No, thank you' but somehow 'Langtons G&T' slipped out instead. At least I didn't say 'large'.

One thing I really appreciate about Karen is that she's the sort of person who needs her own space, and therefore understands other people's need. After spending pretty much all day with her it was nothing personal, I just needed to be on my own for a while – I'm exactly the same with my husband – and I was very glad that she wasn't the sort of person who wanted to be with me the entire time.

We did meet for dinner though, where I thoroughly enjoyed a huge plate of veggie fajitas. I'd been feeling a little out of sorts – possibly the long hike the previous day, maybe the beginnings of a bit of a cold, or perhaps the fact that my blood:alcohol ratio was mostly skewed the wrong way – and I thought a huge dose of vegetables was exactly what I needed. Whatever was wrong I felt much better after dinner, although adding a large glass or two of wine to the day's already extensive alcohol intake, and chatting and laughing with Karen may also have helped. I was mindful that our tour of the Lakes Distillery was first thing the next morning, so I had a large glass of water before I went to bed; as if one glass of water was going to undo the excesses of the rest of the day, but I'm nothing if not optimistic.

Karen

The next morning was the long-awaited Twizy Day!

First, we dropped in to see Alex at Keswick Boot Co. with a pie report, but really we were lusting after trying on some lovely AKU purple boots we'd spotted in the window.

We headed to Keswick Brewing Company and were handed the keys to Tethera, a sort of little motorised tuk tuk disguised as a sheep.

The name Tethera means 'three' and comes from a sheep-counting system called Yan Tan Tethera, which was traditionally used by shepherds in Northern England, especially the Lake District. It goes like this:

> yan, tyan, tethera, methera, pimp, sethera, lethera, hovera, dovera, dick, yan-a-dick, tyan-a-dick, tethra-a-dick, methera-a-dick, bumfit, yan-a-bumfit, tyan-a-bumfit, tethera-a-bumfit, methera-bumfit, giggot.

After a bit of instruction and sorting ourselves out – 'You drive, no you drive'– we hurtled out of the yard and nudged Tethera into the Keswick rush hour. The Twizy has a range of around 35 miles before needing to be recharged, so I kept a careful eye on the battery symbol in the dashboard.

Our first mission was to pootle around in the shadow of Skiddaw. It was two Lakeland locals, Tim Moor and Nick Dymoke-Marr, who discovered that Skiddaw Mountain had an aquifer sitting underneath it. Aquifers are underground rock layers which are saturated with water. Tim and Nick hit upon the idea of pumping this pure and ancient water up to the surface and using it to make a rather unique gin.

Langtons Gin contains 11 botanicals, including juniper, lemon and orange peel, liquorice, and oak bark, which is collected from 100-year-old trees in the Lake District National Park. The gin goes through four distillations before the pure slate-filtered water from the aquifer is added to bring it to 40% ABV.

Before a drop of Langtons had even passed my lips I'd been won

A sheepish Twizy enjoying the view

over by the seriously stylish bottle. The glass is a sort of greeny-grey, just like the slate, the rock, the fells, and so much of the Lakeland landscape, and it's textured with ridges; the contours of Skiddaw.

It was enormous fun zooming round the country roads in Tethera, tooting the little horn to any passers-by. People seemed to love this little sheep as much as we did and were snapping photos of us as we – obviously – whooped and tooted. A van pulled off and rejoined the road twice to get a better look. We couldn't resist taking Tethera on a visit to the splendid Armathwaite Hall, where we were paid back for our cheekiness as Teth (we'd got very friendly) looked a tad sheepish in the car park sitting amongst the sleek sports cars, and Beth nearly lost all her fillings when I hit a hidden speed bump. She pretended to feel dizzy, so we were forced to go in search of cake and hot chocolate.

All too soon it was time to head back, and I wove in and out of the streets and alleys of Keswick, not wanting to panic Beth by letting on that I was lost.

'Isn't this one way?' said Beth.

'Shut up.'

What is it with back seat drivers?

We pulled up outside the brewery. Teth gave a final sad bleat as I walked away.

Keswick Brewing Company is aptly located in Brewery Lane. Sue Jefferson started the brewery with her husband 11 years ago as something to do in her spare time. She was running a B&B at the time, but soon realised that making beer was going to be a full-time job.

The pair sold their B&B and launched into brewing full time.

We joined a small, lively group for a tour led by Keswick Brewing Company's Nigel Green, who was instantly engaging and friendly, still relieved no doubt that Twizy had arrived back in one piece.

Though I like beer very much I didn't really know much about making it. I'd worked through quite a few of those homemade wine kits when I was newly out of university and broke, but my only experience of beer had been in pubs, or when I'd been invited to someone's house and they opened the door and ushered you in with the dreaded words, 'Would you like some of my homebrew?' Any criticism was always received very badly; you'd have fared better by saying one of their children was a spoilt brat than daring to dislike their brew baby.

If you've ever fancied beer making, be prepared to lavish lots of tender loving care until your precious liquid is safely in the casks or bottles. Treat the yeast like a toddler and you won't go far wrong. It frequently plays up during the night, will suddenly demand attention expecting you to drop everything immediately, and refuses to do a thing when you're pressed for time.

Thirst Run was the first beer that Sue and her team made in 2006, and even that was a bit of a surprise. The intended name was First Run, but the labels arrived bearing the name Thirst Run due to a misunderstanding on the phone with the designer.

They now have a whole Thirst range of beers, all made with fell water from Thirlmere.

It does seem that a lot of thought goes into environmental issues here. The vessels are insulated with sheep's wool, every part of the process is carefully monitored to keep an eye on how many chemicals are used, and a regular stream of visitors turn up in the brewery yard – including farmers to collect the sweet, sugary used malt for their cows to eat, and the allotment society who take away the spent hops to sprinkle on their gardens as compost.

Our group arrived back in the cosy bar area; it had to be tasting time.

As Nigel lined up behind the pumps I offered myself up as waitress, recognising that he had quite a few glasses to fill to satisfy us all, and the quicker I could place a glass in each eager hand the

sooner I'd get mine. Obviously the beers were only for the non-drivers. The drivers were supplied with soft drinks to sulk into while us passengers heartily enjoyed the amber nectar. He obviously thought I was made for better things as I was soon promoted to a position behind the bar and tasked with pulling the first pints since my university days. And, I have to tell you, I did the most appalling job. Froth anyone?

Afterwards, we waved our goodbyes – what a fun lot they'd all been! – and jumped on a bus towards Armathwaite Hall, walking the final mile or so in the sunshine.

I know that Beth isn't hugely comfortable in 'posh' hotels, though I really don't know why; she's perfectly well behaved 85% of the time. There're a few things I've come to expect in these places and to me there's no better thrill than finding a little packet of quality biscuits on the coffee tray in the room. And Armathwaite Hall surpassed itself on this count, so as Beth had mooched off to the bar to do some writing (a likely story) I gobbled up the biscuits, nipped out to look around the hotel, and on my return the biscuits had been replenished! A real class act. I was sorely tempted to eat them up and leave the room again, intrigued by how many times I could get away with this… But there was dinner to think about. And my thighs.

After a fabulous soak in the bath I wandered off in search of a G&T, installing myself in the sumptuous lounge and tucking my feet under the sofa to conceal my flip flops.

Spirit/liqueur info sheet

Product	Langtons No.1 Lakeland Gin
Category	Dry Gin 40% ABV
Who makes it?	Nick Dymoke-Marr
When did it start production?	2012
Where is it made?	G&J Distillers, Warrington
Key ingredients	11 botanicals including juniper, lemon and orange peel, liquorice and oak bark
Where can I buy it?	http://www.langtonsgin.co.uk/Home/Main#Stockists

Best way to drink it

Perfect Serve G&T
50ml Langtons Gin
100ml Fentiman's Indian
Tonic Water
Serve in a tall glass with
lots of ice
Lemon slice garnish

Gin Martini
50ml Langtons Gin
5ml Lillet Blanc vermouth
Stir with ice
Pour into a chilled glass
Lemon zest garnish

Perfect Serve
50ml Langtons Gin
Serve in a glass with ice
Lemon zest garnish

Negroni
25ml Langtons Gin
25ml Martini Rosso
vermouth
25ml Campari
Serve in a glass with ice
Orange slice garnish

Gin Martini
65ml Langtons Gin
10ml Noilly Prat dry
vermouth
Stir in -20c thermos with
ice
Serve in a freezer-chilled
glass
Lemon zest garnish

Dry Gin Martini
5ml dry vermouth (pour
the vermouth over a glass
topped with ice then
discard the vermouth
using a strainer)
50ml Langtons Gin
Stir and dilute in ice
Serve in a chilled glass
Lemon zest garnish

Storm chasers

By train	No train service
By bus	A number of bus routes run along the A66 from near the Lakes Distillery to Cockermouth; please check local timetables for more information
By bike	Sustrans Routes 10 and 71 run from near the Lakes Distillery and on into Cockermouth.
By car	From the Lakes Distillery return to the A66 and follow it into Cockermouth
On foot	From Lakes Distillery we followed the local road past Low Field and Dunthwaite, then we forked left to follow the broad path through Hills Wood and down Watch Hill into Cockermouth

Distance = 5.7 miles

DAY TEN: Lakes Distillery to Cockermouth

Beth

Honey is an excellent cure for a hangover. Not that I had one, I'm just saying that if I did happen to have a hangover following an ill-advised combination of beer, gin and wine the day before, then honey would be a good cure for it. And bananas, they're great too, especially when mashed, spread on toast and drizzled with honey. I had to take this hangover curing lark seriously as we had an 11 a.m. appointment to tour the Lakes Distillery and I needed to be in tip-top condition again sharpish.

The one-mile stroll from Armathwaite Hall to the distillery soon blew the last of the cobwebs away and, as the sight of Skiddaw and Bassenthwaite away to the east never fails to lift the spirits, we arrived at the Lakes Distillery bright eyed and bushy tailed.

As soon as we arrived we realised that it's quite a different kettle of fish to the other producers in the county. Where places like Shed 1,

Kin Vodka and Cowmire Hall are tiny operations consisting of one small outbuilding (or shed!), the Lakes Distillery is a large purpose-built brewery and visitors' centre with ample free parking and plenty to see and do.

The distillery sits in a beautifully restored Victorian farm which was renovated by the founder, Paul Currie. The buildings had been empty for 25 years so they pretty much had to start again from scratch, but it's all been sympathetically done and blends in wonderfully with the landscape. They didn't hang around either; the restoration began in spring 2014 and their first spirits were ready in December 2014.

The first things you'll notice when you arrive are the spectacular gates, which capture the logo of the distillery as well as depicting the botanicals used in their spirits.

The tour is thorough and informative, and our guide was clearly knowledgeable and happy to answer any questions we had, though

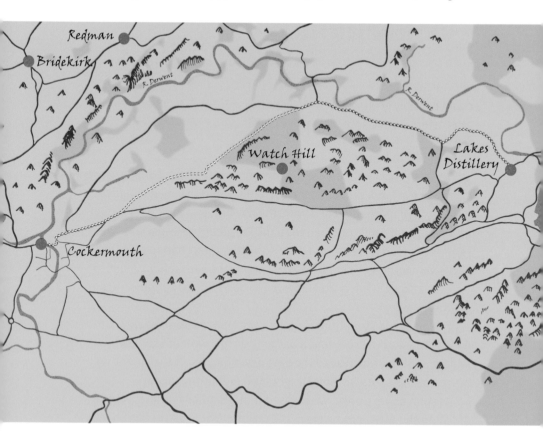

the main question many people appeared keenest to ask was 'when do we get to try some?' Back down in the main visitors' centre they got their answer, as we sampled all three of their main spirits – the cinnamon and angelica in the gin gave it a really warm, rosy feel which went perfectly with the Fever-Tree Indian Tonic water on offer.

We'd come a long way in every sense of the word. At the start of this tour Karen and I would have been happy to grab any old gin, sling in any old tonic and a slice of lemon and call it a G&T, but now we were certified gin snobs and demanded to know which botanicals were used before we selected our tonic and garnish. Seriously, do NOT invite us over for dinner.

With only a five-mile hike ahead of us we weren't in a huge rush, so we hung around for lunch in the Bistro before heading for the hill – literally, we just had one hill to get over and it wasn't even all that high. From the distillery we planned to head up through Setmurthy Plantation and down Watch Hill into Cockermouth; what could possibly go wrong? Well, potentially quite a lot, as the weather forecasters were all predicting doom and gloom with the arrival of the first storm of the year, Aileen. It seems that ever since Michael Fish got it wrong about the storm of 1987 the Met Office have turned erring on the side of caution into an art form and now issue dramatic warnings for any gust of wind strong enough to blow over a plastic picnic chair. (In his defence, Michael Fish did warn about strong winds on that fateful day, he just said there wouldn't be a hurricane which, technically, there wasn't.) Either way the warnings were working and Karen was keen to get the walk done and avoid another soaking.

It was a walk of three distinct sections: tarmac road, woodland and open hillside. The road section was uneventful as we climbed gradually uphill towards Setmurthy Plantation. I'd never been through Setmurthy Woods before but they are definitely somewhere I'll be back to (in fact since completing the walk and writing this book I've already been back twice and dragged my husband along too). Beech trees are less common in Cumbria than in other parts of the

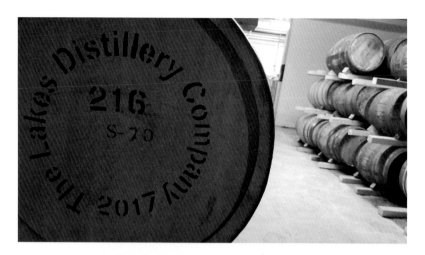

country so it was lovely to see a proper beech woodland; the colours in the autumn are spectacular.

Passing through the gate at the end of the woodland we were treated to breathtaking views in every direction, from the high fells in the south to the sea in the far distance. One thing about having great views is that you can see what weather is approaching and, on this occasion, it looked like Storm Aileen was inbound. I wanted to make the most of the good weather while we had it and take some photos, but Karen was rather more keen to race ahead down the hill in an effort to keep dry. So while I arranged assorted miniatures of alcohol and lead crystal glasses on a nearby dry stone wall, Karen disappeared off into the distance.

I'd not seen the fells from quite this angle before and they looked really dramatic with the menacing clouds hanging around them. Here I was, stood on a hill in the sunshine, while just a few miles away some folks on Grasmoor were probably cursing the wind and the rain. With that in mind I decided it was time to head down too, just in case. The rain eventually caught me towards the bottom of the hill, but it was just a short sharp shower so I was dry again by the time I reached the town.

Cockermouth is another lovely little town and one of the 'undiscovered' gems of north Cumbria. Although it's only a 15-minute drive from Keswick, few visitors make it out here, but those that do are rewarded with a number of very pretty river walks, a wide main street crammed with an array of interesting and independent shops, a brewery (Jennings), a castle and Wordsworth House, where William Wordsworth was born (the town also lays claim to Fletcher Christian, though he was born a few miles away in Eaglesfield).

I explored the high street before tracking Karen down at the B&B, where I dumped my rucksack before heading back out to explore the town and check out the start of tomorrow's route to see just how water logged it was. The B&B was absolutely lovely but a little warm for me – we were sharing a room and I think Karen was quite enjoying a dose of heat, so I left her to enjoy it in peace.

Cockermouth is an ancient town, full of tiny back roads and

Setmurthy Woods, a proper beech woodland

hidden alleyways – my dad always used to call things like that 'secret passages' and I still get a thrill from exploring them, even if they just connect one street of houses with another. One of the back lanes was intriguingly called Teetotal Lane, most likely a reference to one of the many temperance movements in the area, and doubly interesting as it is situated only a few hundred yards from the entrance to Jennings Brewery.

Crossing the river and heading out through Papcastle, I paused to read the information boards, as I knew Karen would have me whizzing straight past them the next day. Cockermouth has a long and fascinating history and Papcastle is built on the site of an old Roman camp, so there have been plenty of interesting finds to examine and write about. The town gets its name from the River Cocker which flows into the River Derwent here, and it's the confluence of the two rivers which has caused problems with flooding in the town in recent years.

I peered into a rain-sodden field full of cows and realised that our original riverside route planned for tomorrow would not be possible – we'd tried a couple of different things but Karen's shoes were remaining resolutely non-waterproof, and hiking with wet feet is no fun, so I headed back to the B&B for a long hot bath and a spot of route rejigging. I may have paused along the way to visit a local pub, but purely for research purposes because I was told it used to be a micro-brewery and I just wanted to check whether it still was. It wasn't, but at least I now knew for certain.

When I got back the heating was still on full, as Karen was trying to dry out her shoes from the soaking on Watch Hill. It wasn't until much later when we decided to try and get some sleep that we realised the radiator was stuck on full blast. By now it was gone 11p.m. and felt a bit late to bother the landlady, so we opened the window and I divided the rest of the night between lying awake worried that someone was going to climb through the window (we were on the ground floor, had we been higher up my only concern would have been Spiderman breaking and entering), and falling asleep and dreaming I was lost in the desert. I blamed the drink. Or at least the lack of it. I wasn't sure I wholly approved of this going to bed sober lark.

Karen

We breakfasted in some style at Armathwaite Hall then trotted off the mile or so to the Lakes Distillery.

It was in the spring of 2014 when Paul Currie came across a dilapidated Victorian farm close to Bassenthwaite Lake and on the banks of the River Derwent. He quickly realised that this derelict building was the perfect setting for a distillery; as part of the father and son team behind the Isle of Arran Distillers, he was no stranger to the whisky business.

Paul wasted no time. Despite strict Lake District listed building rules, the 160-year-old property, which had stood empty for 20 years, opened their doors as the Lakes Distillery just before Christmas 2014.

Beth and I were probably the only visitors arriving on foot that day, which gave us the opportunity to skirt by the field of alpacas and fuss over the babies. I later discovered that this was the Alpacaly Ever After herd, and if it had been a weekend I could have hand fed them with all the other six year olds.

We entered the complex through some fabulously decorative iron gates, created by bespoke metalwork designer Alan Dawson to depict the story of the distillery. Judging by the other visitors coming in from the car park, everyone is bowled over by the sight of them, stopping to trace their fingers over the iron shapes of barley and wheat, and the botanicals juniper, meadowsweet, angelica, heather and hawthorn. An outline of Skiddaw is there too, plus the flowing River Derwent. A four-leaf clover sits atop each gatepost.

We joined the next distillery tour to discover how the Lakes malt whisky, gin and vodka are made.

The lights were lowered in the tour room ready for the video. A helicopter traced the route of the River Derwent from its source at Sprinkling Tarn, winding its way through Keswick and Cockermouth on its journey to the sea 14 miles away at Workington.

'It does tend to rain a lot in the Lake District!' explained our guide. 'Nearby Upper Borrowdale supposedly has the highest levels of rainfall in England. But that means that our lovely River Derwent is full and fast flowing; the waters of the Derwent are continually freshened and flushed through. Pure water makes for a better quality spirit.'

We learnt that Paul Currie's vision was to create one of the leading malt spirits in the world. But you can't rush when it comes to whisky. The Lakes' malt will not be released for general sale until 2019, as the spirit has to spend 3 years and a day maturing in the cask before it can legally be called whisky. And even then no-one can be sure how the whisky will taste. The team can hazard a good guess from the range of casks they've used, but there will still be that element of surprise.

So with the future malt currently maturing – drawing those rich, golden colours and flavours from the casks – the distillery has turned its hand to making a blended whisky, plus vodka and gin.

'The ONE' is the Lakes Distillery's blended whisky featuring whiskies from Scotland, England, Wales and Northern Ireland.

All the spirits here support great causes. The ONE supports Fix the Fells. The Lakes Gin supports the Cumbria Wildlife Trust, while Lakes Vodka supports Great North Ambulance Service.

We followed our guide into the smart and shiny still room.

I found myself standing before a gleaming Susan, with Rachel close behind. Tradition dictates that stills are named after a female; the two whisky stills are named after the wives of the chairman and Paul Currie.

The addition of lights inside the brewing and distilling vessels allows you to peer in and see what's going on inside.

It doesn't take long to distil whisky and although you could drink it straight away, you'd wish you'd waited; it won't be the liquid gold you were hoping for. In the early days of whisky, though, this is exactly what you would have drunk, straight from the still. It wasn't until the 16th century that some hero discovered that whisky kept in oak casks would develop into something far greater.

'Let's go and see the barrels.'

As we filed out of the room we passed Chemmy, the gin and vodka still. This rather beautiful still is like a giant copper onion, with its bulbous bottom tapering away at the top.

Making gin is sort of like adding flavour to vodka. There's always juniper, of course; the other botanicals vary. The still is named after Chemmy Alcock, the champion downhill skier who is very partial to a G&T after a day on the slopes.

Lakes Vodka is triple distilled. In theory the more times you send the alcohol through this process the purer and smoother it will be.

The Lakes Vodka is the only vodka to be distilled on a large scale in the Lake District, and the same goes for the gin.

We were now gathering in the distillery's warehouse, where the casks of malt whisky were lined up waiting to mature.

It's when you pour whisky into a wooden barrel that things start to get interesting.

By law, Scottish whisky is made in oak casks, but south of the border a variety of casks can be and are used. Lakes distillery are experimenting with American oak, bourbon barrels, Spanish oak and Oloroso sherry casks. These casks impart a whole range of flavours to the whisky, such as vanilla, sultanas, raisins, candied-peel, cinnamon, nutmeg and caramel.

As is only fitting, the tour concludes in the tasting room (no pushing, please) where you are given the chance to sample some of the products.

First up was the blended whisky, The ONE.

We were going to check out its legs. We swirled our glasses, coating their walls with whisky, then watched as the spirit ran back down the glass. This is called the 'legs'. Younger and lighter whiskies have thin legs that run quickly. More mature and heavier whiskies have slower, thicker legs. Bit like me, really.

The liquid slipped across my tongue, a deliciously warm burn rolling down my throat. To my inexperienced palate it was woody, smoky and very smooth. All I knew for sure was that I liked it.

By the time I opened my eyes (it's important to give yourself over completely to the experience) there was a tot of gin coming my way. The mix includes 14 botanicals, 6 of which are local to the Lakes, including Cumbrian juniper. Fresh, citrusy and definitely moreish. An optional bottle of tonic was being passed around too but I was more than happy to drink this gin neat.

All too soon we were on to our final tasting. Lakes Vodka is made from wheat and, as you already know, from lashings of water from the River Derwent. I'd been thinking about this during our trip. When you're making spirits, how much does the water source really matter? Quite a bit, I would have thought. With Lakes Distillery using water from the River Derwent surely that's got to be a big plus point? I mean, look at the huge difference in the taste of water from different sources, and even different parts of the country. And Derwent water is pure. On a scale from 0-100%, where zero is absolutely pure, the water from the River Derwent comes in at a very impressive 0.6%.

So, to the vodka. There are those who insist that vodka is misunderstood. Abused even. Before my Polish daughter-in-law took me in hand I'd never even tasted vodka without a mixer added. But today I would. The Lakes Vodka was incredibly smooth and silky with a little welcome heat. Which was just the job to fire me up for the short 5-mile hike to Cockermouth.

The rain held off as we began with a little road walking, then a beautiful forest trail took us up into hills.

Beth was in a photo-snapping mood, while I was more interested in the black rain clouds which were rapidly rolling in towards us. The distant hills were already shrouded in a dense grey mist. I forged on ahead through fields of sheep, my eyes on the just visible traffic snaking along the narrow strip of road which led into Cockermouth. I made it to the road just before the heavens opened and stopped under a bus shelter to don rain gear and waterproof my backpack, before splashing on towards Cockermouth and the enticing prospect of a warm and cosy B&B. I wasn't going anywhere that evening aside from a dash into the supermarket for essential rations.

There was a tap on the door as I was about to tear into my goodies.

'Just to let you know,' said the landlady, 'Storm Aileen is coming in. We're under flood watch.'

I went online to the Met Office: 'Met Office issues weather warnings for Cumbria as Storm Aileen threatens winds of up to 75mph.'

Apparently, so the site told me, people take a lot more notice of a storm if it's given a name. People don't do a great deal when warned of bad weather but will take much more action to avoid Angus, Barbara, Conor and Doris, the first few storms of last year. Something caught my eye: 'Storm names for 2017/2018 announced'.

I still can't decide if I'm thrilled or horrified that the storm denoted by the letter 'K' this coming year is to be named Storm Karen. Suffice to say, there'll be hell to pay when we get to K!

Spirit/liqueur info sheet

Product	The Lakes Distillery Gin, Vodka and The ONE British blended whisky
Category	Gin: London Dry Gin 43.7% ABV Vodka: 40% ABV Whisky: 40% ABV
Who makes it?	The Lakes Distillery
When did it start production?	2014
Where is it made?	Near Bassenthwaite Lake
Key ingredients	The ONE: A blend of whiskies from around the British Isles, each with their own distinctive characteristics. Gin: 14 botanicals including juniper, bilberry, heather, hawthorn, mint, coriander seed, angelica root, orris root, liquorice, lemon and orange peel Vodka: made from English wheat
Where can I buy it?	https://www.lakesdistillery.com

Best way to drink it

The ONE
Enjoy as you please, neat or over ice. Add a little water to release the flavours and aroma for maximum enjoyment

Whisky Smash
Chilled whisky glass
50ml The ONE Whisky
1 lime cut into small wedges
1 cup diced cucumber
5 sprigs fresh mint plus more for garnish
Ice
100ml cold limeade
Combine the lime, cucumber and mint in the glass. Stir to release flavours.
Fill the glass with ice and pour in the whisky.
Top off with limeade
Garnish with fresh mint, a wedge of lime and a wheel of cucumber

Old Fashioned
Chilled old fashioned glass
2 shots of The ONE whisky
2 dashes of Angostura bitters
1 teaspoon of brown sugar
Few dashes of plain water
Place the sugar in the glass and saturate with the Angostura bitters, add a dash of plain water and muddle until dissolved.
Fill your glass with ice cubes and add your shots of The ONE Whisky
Garnish with an orange slice

Manhattan cocktail
60ml The ONE Whisky by the Lakes Distillery
20ml sweet vermouth
2 dashes orange bitters
Combine The ONE whisky & sweet vermouth
Add orange bitters
Stir and pour over ice
Garnish with lemon twist

Lakes Blood and Sand
25ml The ONE whisky
25ml sweet vermouth
25ml cherry liqueur
35ml orange juice
Add all ingredients to a shaker, shake fast for 10–15 seconds, and pour into a martini glass. Rimming the glass with sugar is optional, depending on your preference. Garnish with an orange and enjoy!

Gin
Try with a slice of pink grapefruit and a light premium tonic.

The Lakes Bramble
50ml Lakes Gin
25ml lemon juice
12.5ml sugar syrup
10ml Crème De Mure
Shake first 3 ingredients and strain over crushed ice. Drizzle with Crème de Mure.
Garnish with a slice of lemon and a blackberry.

English 75 Cocktail
Chilled champagne glass
1 shot of The Lakes Gin
2 shots of preferred English sparkling wine
½ shot of lemon juice
2 dashes of simple syrup
Combine The Lakes Gin, syrup and lemon juice in a cocktail shaker filled with ice. Shake vigorously and strain into an iced champagne class. Top up your drink with fizz and stir gently
Garnish with a twist of lemon

Lavender Collins
50ml The Lakes Gin
25ml lemon juice
15ml lavender sugar
Soda water
Combine the gin, lemon juice and sugar
Shake, pour over ice and top up with soda water
Garnish with a sprig of lavender

Vodka

Drink neat over ice or in a cocktail of your choice.

Grapefruit and Thyme Smash (serves 1)
Glass/ice
Jam jar
Crushed Ice
50ml Lakes Vodka
75ml grapefruit juice
25ml lemon juice
50ml sugar syrup
Method/strain
Combine the Lakes Vodka, grapefruit juice, lemon and sugar syrup in a cocktail shaker.
Shake!
Garnish with 2 sprigs of thyme

Winter Berry Martini (Serves 1)
Martini glass
50ml Lakes Vodka
50ml cranberry juice
25ml sweet vermouth
Dash of Angostura bitters
Combines the Lakes Vodka, cranberry juice, bitters and sweet vermouth in a cocktail glass, shake and pour over ice cubes
Garnish with cranberries

Vesper (Serves 1)
Chilled coupe glass
1 shot of Lakes Vodka
2 shots of Lakes Gin
Half a shot of Lillet Blanc
Simply pour your spirits into a cocktail shaker filled with ice and strain into a chilled glass
Garnish with a twist of lemon

From the sauce to the sea

By train	No train service between Cockermouth and Workington but there's a regular service between Workington and Whitehaven
By bus	A number of bus routes run along the A66 from Cockermouth to Workington and from Workington to Whitehaven, please check local timetables for more information
By bike	Sustrans Route 71 runs from Cockermouth to Workington then route 72 down to Whitehaven.
By car	Follow the A66 from Cockermouth to Workington then the A595 and A596 to Whitehaven
On foot	We left Cockermouth through Papcastle then continued along the road through Great Broughton to Camerton, where we crossed the footbridge to Great Clifton. We then continued along the local road to Stainburn and on into Workington and through the town to the coast and station.

Distance = 12 miles

Another wonky horizon, in Workington

DAY ELEVEN: Cockermouth to Whitehaven

Beth

Our last hike. Tomorrow we'll visit The Rum Story in Whitehaven then get the train home, so this was our last proper hiking day. The time has absolutely flown by and I feel quite proud of the distance we've covered; Ulverston feels like a long way away right now. Today the original plan was to make it as far as The Old Ginn House Inn in Great Clifton, then catch the bus to Workington and the train from there to Whitehaven, but things didn't quite work out that way.

   As well as packing our rucksacks on autopilot we were now also a little like an old married couple when it came to getting ready in the mornings – we knew each other's routine and went through the motions of boiling the kettle and filling the flasks pretty much without thinking. Given the hot and sticky conditions in the room overnight I was very glad to get out into the fresh morning air, even if it was drizzling a little. I was also glad I'd checked out the start of the

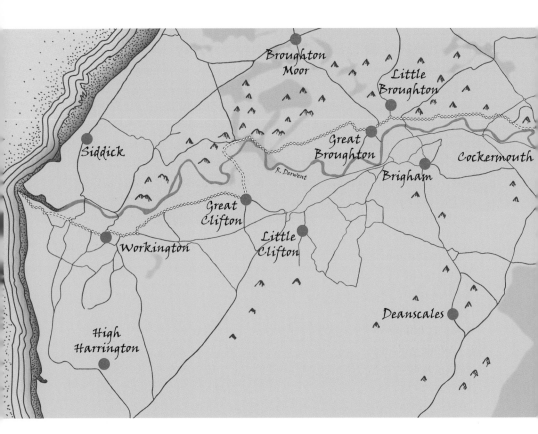

route the night before so I could relax and enjoy the stroll through the town.

Karen was horrified at the height of the floods (marked on a wall in the town); it really was hard to imagine how devastating they'd been and how quickly Cockermouth had got back on its feet again. Storm Desmond swept through Cumbria on 5th and 6th December 2015, flooding the town and wiping out much of the high street, and yet on 12th December the town had welcomed over 10,000 people to its annual food festival. A few businesses sadly failed to recover, but overall Cockermouth bounced back with a resilience you have to admire.

Our route wound out through Great Broughton, where we paused outside the post office in the sunshine for a slurp of tea and a biscuit. We'd cunningly figured out how to guarantee good weather: we put the waterproof covers on our rucksacks and donned our waterproof jackets from the start. Nothing is better guaranteed to ward off rain than properly prepared hikers.

At Camerton we crossed a footbridge over to Great Clifton – the original had been washed away in the floods of 2009 (before they began naming storms) but the replacement had withstood the worst Storm Desmond had to throw at it and showed no signs of going anywhere. We located The Old Ginn House in the heart of the village but were disappointed to learn it had nothing at all to do with alcohol and a lot to do with horses and grain production (to be fair, gin requires grain so we weren't a million miles away). The original 17th-century farm is now a rather nice-looking inn and restaurant where they do serve gin, they just don't make it.

It was only just lunchtime and our legs were still feeling pretty fresh, so we paused briefly for a bite to eat – which began on a nice bench near the crossroads and finished in a bus stop when the rain came – before continuing our journey on to Workington (after the rain stopped again), thereby allowing us to follow the Derwent from Lakes Distillery all the way to the sea.

While walking along roads is easy enough, it was enormously disappointing to see the amount of litter strewn in the hedgerows – when we drive by it's easy to miss, but walking past means you get to see it all and there was no way we could have collected everything we saw. It wasn't just the main roads either, although they were the worst; many of the tiny country lanes we followed had Costa cups and McDonald's wrappers stuck in the hedges, and we spotted carrier bags high up in a number of trees. It really was deeply depressing and made me realise how far we still have to go to educate some people about the impact we're having on the environment.

Workington town is actually quite a long way from the railway station and shoreline (there used to be another station in the centre of town but that has long since closed). We did consider stopping at the station but that would have felt wrong, so we continued on all the way to the very end of the jetty – to go any further would have required swimsuits. From there we could see clear across the Solway to southern Scotland, which may have had more whisky than we did but was also getting a lot more rain too, by the looks of it.

The jetty marks the start (or end) point of one of the coast to coast cycle routes and, with our enormous rucksacks, a few people mistook us for C2C'ers and shouted their congratulations. Although we'd not covered the same distance as someone completing the Coast to

Coast, we had come a long way in the previous 10 days and this was the very end of the hiking part of our journey. While, strictly speaking, we didn't deserve those specific congratulatory comments, we did feel chuffed that we'd achieved something almost as impressive, so we simply smiled and waved back.

As we stood on the end of the jetty, it seemed only fitting that we celebrate our achievement in some small way, so I called Karen over, fished a couple of miniatures of Strawberry Bank's Strawberry Vodka out of my rucksack (stashed there since I'd acquired them in Bowness while Karen was distracted with a pasty) and suggested we celebrate. Although we still had the gorgeous Cumbria Crystal glasses in our packs we were too tired to dig them out so, like the classy pair we are, we unscrewed the caps, chinked bottles and downed them in one. We'd come a very long way since our sophisticated first night in Virginia House; our spirits were still high, but our standards had clearly fallen.

Workington has many claims to fame but the one which intrigued me the most was the connection to Mary Queen of Scots, simply for the precision shown in the commemorative plaque on the quayside. It marks the spot where Mary, having fled Scotland across the Solway, came ashore on 15th May 1568 at 7 p.m. – how precise is that? I couldn't tell you the exact time we saw the plaque but they know to the minute what time she landed there 500 or so years ago.

The train journey to Whitehaven was swift and uneventful and we were soon picking our way through the town in search of our B&B. I've never made any secret of the fact that I have an enormous soft spot for Whitehaven; it has a fascinating history, a beautiful harbour and spectacular views across to Scotland. Our B&B was a little out of town and we knew it was going to be an adventure from the moment we rang the doorbell...

It sounded as if we'd awoken the hounds of hell, who promptly raced to the door, hotly pursued by a screaming landlady. Karen looked rather apprehensive. The landlady's face appeared around the door.

'Are you okay with dogs?'

'No,' replied Karen

'Oh...' pause '...wait there then.'

She then proceeded to lock one dog (some sort of wolfhound cross) in the breakfast room and shooed the other one (an adorable but out of control Staffie cross) away down the corridor. We entered nervously and she showed us to our rooms – separate rooms this time so I could give Karen a break from my snoring.

When she told Karen that she didn't do porridge for breakfast because 'no one ever asks for it' we knew we were in for an interesting time. To be fair, the place looked as if it had been fairly recently decorated, but the stairs were thick with dog hairs and our rooms, although clean, weren't sparkly and I had a resident spider in my bathroom who, judging by the state of his web, had been in residence for a while. Please don't get me wrong, I absolutely love dogs, but if you're operating a business that's open to the public the dogs need to be under control, and the hairs on the carpet certainly need to be hoovered up from time to time.

I put my feet up on the bed, reached into my rucksack for my Cumbria Crystal glass and a handful of miniatures from Lakes Distillery, and poured myself a drink or two as I pondered our achievement. From something that had started as a mad idea on a fell, here I now was, having completed all the walking and on the verge of heading home. I'm a sucker for all those 'just go for it' memes on the internet, but I really had just 'gone for it,' and it seemed to

be working out rather well – people on social media had followed our updates and blogs, we'd made new friends, discovered new bits of the county and sampled (and enjoyed!) just about every variation of spirit the county had to offer.

Cumbria Crystal glass intact at Whitehaven!

Feeling rather chuffed with ourselves we headed down into Whitehaven, where I planned to introduce Karen to the excellent local chippy, and a shelter on the harbour which me and Steve had christened the 'chippy hut,' on account of the fact that it's not too far from the chippy and offers protection both from the elements and from the chip-pilfering gulls around the harbour walls.

We made it to the chippy just before they closed and my manners completely let me down – they only had one fish and I bagged it without asking, or even thinking of, Karen. I honestly didn't twig what I'd done until after the hike was over and I was going back over my notes and recalling the events of the day. Maybe it was because I was overly tired and hungry, or maybe it was because I'd already had a couple of medicinal gins, but either way it was very rude. Karen, I am sorry and I owe you a fish.

With my ill-gotten fish and the smell of salt and vinegar in our nostrils we headed for the chippy hut. I like to think Karen was impressed with the hut – okay, so perhaps that wasn't its intended purpose, but it was the perfect place to hoover up our chips and reflect back over our hike.

As we returned towards to the B&B I suggested perhaps celebrating the end of our hike with a drink, but Karen was tired and wanted to head back, so we compromised and took a detour via a supermarket where I bought a celebratory night cap – one of those 'today is the end of the holiday so I may as well have another few drinks as I'm back home tomorrow' moments. All I had to do in the morning was survive breakfast (which turned out to be no mean feat!) and be lucid enough to enjoy our final stop at The Rum Story – piece of cake. Or piece of Cumberland Rum Nicky to be precise.

Karen

That night, Beth struggled. The radiator in our room appeared to have two settings: scorching or roasting. And Beth was doing both. I just dreamt I was back in the Med.

After visiting Lakes Distillery yesterday and hearing how they use the water from the River Derwent to make their spirits, we thought we'd leave Cockermouth today and follow the river the 12 miles to

Workington, where it flows into the Irish Sea.

Last night, yet again, I'd over estimated my alcohol-imbibing ability so I had to find space in my pack for an unopened bottle of red wine. I would discard most of my stuff before leaving that behind. We covered our packs and ourselves from head to toe and prepared for another day battling foul weather. The first thing I saw as we left Cockermouth was a little patch of blue sky. And as we walked on, it grew bigger. And bigger. By late morning we were sitting in the sunshine eating cake outside a little village post office.

There was more good news to come. After all those days of squeaky backpack, it had stopped! Ceased!

'Well, what's different?' asked Beth. 'What have you changed?'

'Nothing that I can think of... except... well, all I've done that's different is shove in a bottle of wine. That must be the answer then! I'll never hike again without a bottle of good Côtes Du Rhône.'

And from that moment on, I didn't hear another squeak.

On a whim we decided to seek out a pub in Great Clifton with an intriguing name, The Old Ginn House Inn. A quick foray into the reception area explained it all. The main bar in the pub was the ginn room after which the inn had been named. This was a unique rounded room where, in times past, horses walked around turning a grindstone to crush the crops. This was known as 'ginning'.

Not quite our idea of ginning, then.

I knew that when we reached Workington the plan was to catch a train the few miles to Whitehaven, our next night stop. I also knew that before we did this we'd have to find the pier and go right to the end of it. If there's 'the end of', 'the top of' or 'the bottom of' then Beth just has to go there; to the farthest, the highest, the lowest point. As we walked out along the pier folk kept asking, 'Are you starting or finishing?'

I was puzzled. 'Er ... finishing'.

'Oh well done! Fantastic!'

'Well, thank you!'

It wasn't until we reached the end of the jetty that I saw the big plaque and realised it was the start/finish point of one of the impressively long distance Coast to Coast cycle routes – there are 3 altogether, but some folks still walk the cycle route. Nutters.

'Well done!'

'Thank you! Thanks very much!'

What a fraud. Good job they didn't ask to see our bikes.

'Well, maybe as everyone is congratulating us, we should celebrate,' mused Beth.

'Definitely! How?'

I followed her up the steps, which went up then wrapped around the concrete hut at the end of the pier. The wind was howling, our coats flapping wildly, hair whipping across our faces. The sea tumbled below us, a murky, muddy brown. Beth popped a little bottle into my palm and I quickly snapped my fingers around it to foil the wind, which was snatching at anything not bolted down.

I shuffled along and made sure I was standing by the big C2C sign attached to the hut (show off) and we clinked our dinky bottles; a glance at the label told me it was Strawberry Bank Vodka. Just the job. I twisted off the bottle cap and poured the sweet, red liquid into my mouth, accompanied by several clumps of unwanted hair. The effect was deliciously fruity, scented like a punnet of berries (the drink) and horribly stringy (the hair).

We bought a couple of tickets at Workington Station and had around 20 minutes to lose before our train arrived. Beth went straight onto the platform to cool down and I huddled in the waiting room and activated a gel hand warmer. I'd forgotten to tell Beth but the previous night I'd read about a woman who'd been barred from boarding her train because she had some booze in her luggage. Northern Rail were having a bit of a crackdown to try and reduce antisocial behaviour on the Whitehaven–Carlisle service and had introduced a 'dry trains policy'. From what I could gather, it seemed to apply to late night weekend trains and Beth and I were weekday afternoon travellers. But with a rucksack groaning with bottles wrapped in underwear and old socks and a cut crystal glass to go with them, I naturally looked as guilty as hell. I had to give up the

Great Clifton – look out for the Old Ginn House Inn in the village

toasty waiting room in the end and go in search of Beth on the platform, as the chap in the ticket office would not stop staring. *He knew.*

We jumped on the train for the short journey to Whitehaven, my backpack swinging into the door and resounding with an enormous clink.

Beth had been telling me how the town was used as a template for the expansion of New York during the 18th century. As we walked through the streets I could see exactly what she meant. I've always found it really easy to find my way around Manhattan, as it's laid out in a grid pattern. The avenues run north to south and the streets east to west. It's so logical. Whitehaven may be a fraction of the size but its streets are laid out in the same way.

Looking at the harbour packed with local yachts and small pleasure boats, it's hard to believe that Whitehaven was once such an important port, on a par with Bristol and Liverpool. I loved the names around here: Sugar Tongue Quay, Lime Tongue Quay. You can just imagine sugar and limes being slurped up and rolled via giant tongues on or off the docked ships.

We headed away from the water in search of our B&B, which looked worryingly deserted as we approached. Our fears were unfounded, though, as a quick press on the doorbell brought what sounded like an entire pack of dogs to the other side of the door. The door was opened a crack.

'You don't mind dogs, do you?'

'Well...er...how many of them?'

'Wait. I'll put them away.'

The mob howled in frustration as we finally entered the hallway and they were unable to sink their teeth into our ankles.

The landlady was perplexed. 'There should be three of you.'

'Er, no. Just us!'

'No. There definitely should be three of you.'

'Well, I'm not sure we can do much about that.'

'I was expecting three! Oh well, I suppose you'd better come up.' It was all highly unsatisfactory but we were eventually shown our rooms.

I was just about to flop on the bed when there was a tap on my door.

It was the landlady. 'Forgot to tell you something. Come into the bathroom.'

She then went to great lengths to make sure I understood that under no circumstances must I put any sanitary items in the toilet.

She brought her face within inches of mine and raised a querying eyebrow.

'You do understand? *Absolutely nothing.* And especially none of those...'

'Wait!' I interrupted. 'I've got it. It's fine. It won't be a problem.'

'Well, if you're sure.'

I was sure; I'm 56 years old. She seemed oblivious to my giant boxes of Menopause Support Plus and Osteocare standing on the shelf right by her arm.

Finally, she left me to my own devices and I pulled everything out of my pack in search of an item I knew was squashed somewhere down there at the bottom. I was going to celebrate the end of all the hiking by wearing a dress.

And now one of the moments that Beth had been waiting for. A visit to a renowned fish and chip shop in Whitehaven. It could have all gone so horribly wrong when it appeared that the 'fab chippy' had run out of, er, fish and chips, but they did somehow manage to scrape together one portion of fish and chips and an extra bag of chips. I let Beth have the fish and chips. Well, she had been talking about them since last year.

She'd also been insisting that there was only one place to eat them and that was in Whitehaven's 'chippy hut,' so off we went. As it turned out, it wasn't a seaweed-stinky, dank, wooden shed on a windswept cliff as I'd imagined, but a multi-million pound crow's nest structure bang in the harbour.

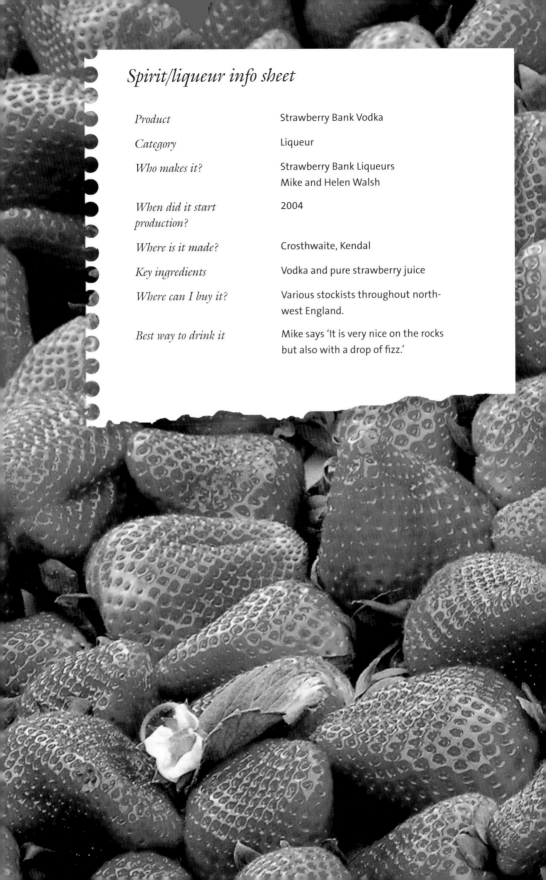

Spirit/liqueur info sheet

Product	Strawberry Bank Vodka
Category	Liqueur
Who makes it?	Strawberry Bank Liqueurs Mike and Helen Walsh
When did it start production?	2004
Where is it made?	Crosthwaite, Kendal
Key ingredients	Vodka and pure strawberry juice
Where can I buy it?	Various stockists throughout north-west England.
Best way to drink it	Mike says 'It is very nice on the rocks but also with a drop of fizz.'

Homeward bound

By train   Regular train service connects the towns

By bus   A number of bus routes run from Whitehaven to Ulverston but you will need to make connections, please check local timetables for more information

By bike   Sustrans Route 72 will take you part of the way but you'll then need to use main roads to complete the route

By car   Follow the A595 to Grizebeck then the A5092 and the A590 to Ulverston

On foot   The England Coast Path/ Cumbria Coastal Way will lead you back to Ulverston – a 2 to 3 day hike depending on level of fitness

DAY TWELVE: Whitehaven to Ulverston

Beth

I know Karen had a particularly interesting time at the B&B with the landlady bellowing outside her door from 6:45 a.m., but I'll leave her to tell you that story. I was tucked away on the top floor so sadly missed all the fun.

It's hard to know what the real highlight of breakfast was: the do-it-yourself bacon sarnie, the lack of decaff (which 'no-one ever asks for') which resulted in me scampering back up 3 floors to retrieve a sachet I'd bought with me, and arriving breathless back in the breakfast room to be met by the landlady saying, 'oh yes, I do have some of those somewhere in the kitchen', or having to remove sharp objects from within Karen's reach because I wasn't sure how far the 'no white bread' discussion was going to go.

Oddly, the thing which sticks most in my mind was the painting, hanging above our breakfast table, of the Mona Lisa which was being defaced by trolls. It was interesting enough as it was but when the landlady switched it on causing the trolls to mechanically leap

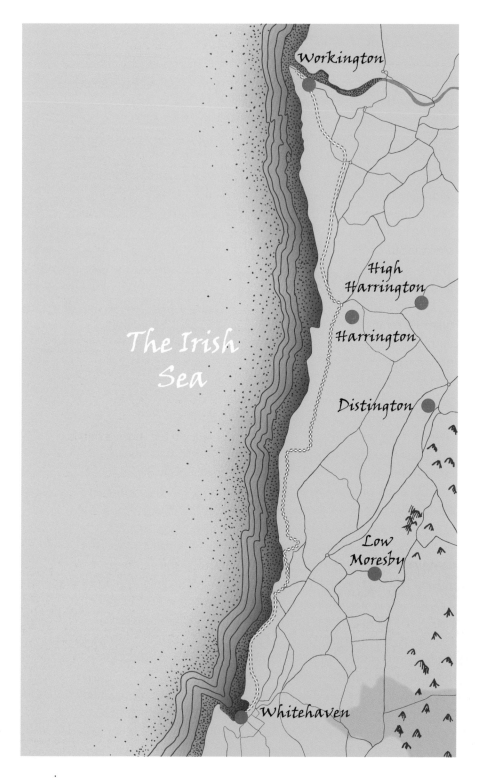

Workington

High
Harrington

The Irish
Sea

Harrington

Distington

Low
Moresby

Whitehaven

into life with their marker pens and white paint, it truly came into its own. I've never seen anything quite like it and couldn't decide if I absolutely loved its quirky weirdness or hated its tackiness. I think the safest thing to say is that I think it was a fun thing to look at in someone else's home, but I don't think I'd want it in mine.

Having been tipped off by Karen regarding the demands to pay in cash I politely explained that carrying that amount of money around when we were hiking wouldn't have been wise or safe, and if she'd mentioned it the night before we'd have happily picked up some cash while we were in town. Although it was all irritating at the time, looking back now I feel quite sorry for the landlady; we got the feeling she was out of her depth a little and could probably use another pair of hands around the place; it had the makings of a great B&B but it did need a little more customer focus.

Our first, and only, stop of the day was The Rum Story, and their premises reminded me a lot of the TARDIS. The deceptively small entrance off the street opens up and expands around you the further back you go. It's nice and cheap to get in and once inside you're free to explore the courtyards, cellars and 3 floors of exhibits. We'd managed to tag on to a guided tour so got a little bit of extra special treatment, but there's plenty to do for any visitor and, despite being an alcohol-based attraction, there's loads to keep kids engaged too, as the exhibits don't just focus on the rum but tell the history of Whitehaven too.

The story goes all the way back to the 1700s and traces the history of the Jefferson family, as well as Whitehaven's connection to shipping and the slave trade. The Jefferson clerk's office looked for all the world as if someone had just stepped away for their lunch,

allowing us visitors to explore in their absence – in reality, the office closed in 1998 and nothing in there has been touched since.

Beyond that there's a rainforest room and the old vaults, as well as specially built exhibits bringing to life the trading history of the town, the rum-making process and the social impact of rum on the country, including a colourful visit to the London 'punch' houses. where guests were liberally dosed with rum before being taken advantage of by some of the local 'ladies'. On the top floor you'll find stories of pirates, rum smuggling and prohibition, as well as a selection of rum cocktail recipes – and all this from one small doorway off the main street.

At the end of the tour we enjoyed a sample of the rum – wonderful and warming, and I made sure I bought a bottle to pop in my hot chocolate later (which I'm pretty sure doesn't count as alcohol when it's in a warm milky drink). We also loaded up with rum butter and tea cake made with rum-soaked fruit (definitely doesn't count). I had hoped to get my hands on some of their famous Cumberland Rum Nicky – something which so impressed Paul Hollywood when he visited in 2013 that he included it in one of the 'technical challenge' rounds in the 2017 season of Great British Bake Off, much to the confusion of the bakers, none of whom had ever heard of it – but sadly they were out of stock. Great excuse to go back!

We wandered out of The Rum Story and into the sunshine; funny how now all the hiking was over the sun had decided to make an appearance. With the sun shining down on us and a couple of hours to kill before our train home, we took a stroll around Whitehaven, specifically the harbour, which I absolutely adore. About half way round town I realised I'd left my hiking pole behind at The Rum Story – for one desperate moment we were worried I'd left it at the B&B (I'd left my pole in a few places during our journey) – but thankfully the lovely Angela was looking after it for me in the shop. I was also concerned that Karen may be getting justifiably irritated with me leaving my pole behind yet again but, to be frank, the sun was shining so she really didn't care.

I don't think either of us would have said we were worn out by our adventure, but we were rather weary, so we settled down in a harbour-front cafe for a cup of tea while we waited for our train home. Rather than being euphoric at our achievement I think we were both a little subdued; perhaps it was tiredness or maybe it was the fact that, despite having gotten along perfectly well for the previous 12 days, we were both now ready to enjoy our own space again.

Pausing at Tesco for Karen to grab a last few snacks for our ride home, we headed to the station where, as luck would have it, another Twitter friend

Rum place, Whitehaven!

I'd never previously met turned out to be the train driver. I love the way social media keeps surprising me like that.

If you've not taken the train around the Cumbrian coast then you're really missing out; it's one of the finest railway journeys in the UK. For the full coastal experience take the train from Arnside to Carlisle – the journey lasts over 3 hours but the views are spectacular, with seascapes dominating the western views and the fells of the Lake District rising up in the east. The route was originally built to support and connect the mining and other industries in Barrow, Whitehaven and Workington with the rest of the UK, but as cheap imports grew, so those industries declined and closed, and now it is pretty much exclusively a passenger route.

We were only doing a relatively short hop from Whitehaven back through Ulverston to my home in Grange-over-Sands, but we managed to bag a good window seat and both of us thoroughly enjoyed the views as the train wound its way south past Ravenglass, around Black Combe (one of my absolutely favourite fells) and through Barrow. When we stopped at Ulverston I jumped out to take a photo to commemorate us coming full circle; I know I could have popped back to take the photo at a later date but that wouldn't have seemed right.

Arriving back into Grange it felt a little odd to be home. Steve was out, so, without any real ceremony or celebration, we sorted through the various bags we'd sent home with our faithful Gin Sherpa and Karen packed her rucksack one last time before loading everything into her car and heading off. It was less than two weeks since we'd first met but we'd done such a lot during that time that it felt as if we'd known each other a lot longer.

As with every adventure there had been some fabulous highs and some challenging lows, but we'd got through it all in one piece, met many fascinating people along the way, and now had a proper story to tell. We may not have conquered the South Pole but we created and completed our very own Cumbrian adventure, and I was certainly very proud of the pair of us.

I looked at my drinks cabinet, which was now crammed with a vast array of colourful spirits and liqueurs, ran a hot bath and poured myself a large G&T. Some people have asked me if I'm now sick of gin, but far from it; I am a fan for life and fear that my gin snobbery is only just getting started.

Karen

Next morning, I was woken up sharp at 6.45 a.m. by the B&B landlady, who was full-throatedly yelling outside my room. I would've opened the door but her dog was flinging his rump at it.

'Wait!'

'No, please, it's fine. No worries!' a male voice rang out. I heard what I imagined was him stumbling into the bannister in an attempt to get away.

'No wait!' she insisted. 'I'll have another look for your underpants. Are you sure I had them?'

It seems she'd done some washing for him and certain items had gone astray.

When we emerged from our rooms she was waiting for us in the empty breakfast room. The night before, she'd asked what we'd like for our breakfast and I'd asked if I could have porridge.

'No. It's the first time I've ever been asked. Nobody ever wants it.'

Beth ordered a bacon sandwich. It was possible, our landlady agreed, but only if she brought bread and bacon on a plate and Beth put it together herself.

So, seated in the breakfast room, we ordered coffee.

'Decaff, please,' said Beth.

'No decaff as nobody ever wants it,' she replied – i.e. 'You two are weird.'

She ranted about the failings of Whitehaven for half an hour while we patiently waited for her to get our breakfast. Eventually we had to remind her.

'Oh! The bacon sandwich! I'd forgotten!'

'Do *you* want anything?' she challenged me.

'White toast please.'

'No white toast, nobody ever wants it.'

I'd had enough. 'I want white toast.'

We squared up. Eventually she flounced from the room and came back with a lump of frozen bread which she stuffed into the microwave.

Mercifully, it was check out time.

'Cash only,' she said.

'No,' I said.

'I only take cash.'

'Well, I can't pay then. You should have said.'

I got a look which ought to have turned me to stone and she stomped off, returning shortly after with a cash machine.

While I was paying the phone rang. She grabbed it. 'Who is it?'

I could make out a chap's voice enquiring about making a group booking.

'You'll have to phone back. I'm in the middle of breakfast.'

'What time shall I call back?'

'What? Oh erm… half an hour… wait… Look, I'm very busy. Go away!'

With that, she slammed the phone down.

We left to head to The Rum Story.

This museum is set in the very premises where Robert and Henry Jefferson ran their empire and it's been beautifully staged; there's the bonded warehouses, the cellars and courtyards, and the original clerk's office with its heavy wooden desks, old-fashioned safe and handwritten logbooks.

We joined a tour and all shuffled into the clerk's office, where I admired the attention to detail.

'I used to have boxes and boxes of those,' said a chap beside me, pointing towards the beautifully old-fashioned door handles. 'From my work.'

'They're lovely,' I said. 'What happened to them?'

'Threw them all away. Worth a bomb now.'

He shook his head, and to avoid dwelling on the small fortune he'd binned, transferred his attention to the tour guide who was ushering us on.

Our journey continued through a Caribbean rainforest and from there the rum story began.

Whitehaven was involved in the slave trade and was one of the country's busiest ports in the 18th century. Ships left with cargoes of cotton, fleeces and pulses bound for West Africa. Once there, the goods were exchanged for slaves who were transported to the West Indies where they were put to work on the sugar plantations. The ship was loaded with sugar, spices and rum and sailed back to Whitehaven.

The Jefferson family owned some of these sugar plantations and 12 sailing ships.

Rum has long been linked with the sea. Imagine, if you will, a life in the Royal Navy of old; wrestling with complex knots, shimmying up the rigging and staggering around with kegs of gunpowder. Now imagine doing that after downing a hefty measure of eye-wateringly strong rum.

For over 300 years, a daily booze ration was an essential part of life in the Royal Navy. And it went on until fairly recently, when someone decided that it really wasn't a good idea for folk to be operating high-tech equipment and be exposed to nuclear technologies after quaffing the best part of half a pint of rum.

On 31st July 1970, now known as Black Tot Day, the very last rum rations were dished out to the British Royal Navy. Ships mourned this darkest of days in various ways. Black armbands were worn, rum tots were thrown overboard, and HMS *Dolphin* really went to town with drummers and pipers accompanying a coffin.

The tour continued. Not being very creative when it comes to artistic ability, I was full of admiration for *Rusties Rum Fun Room*, a miniature recreation of a bar housed in a glass cabinet. The chequered floor tiling was an old draughts board, there was a Wurlitzer jukebox made with an egg slicer, bar pumps made with wine stoppers and shiny CD table tops. You really have to peer in to appreciate it. Its creator found a use for all sorts of things: golf tees, clothes pegs, hair combs, tiny chess pieces, bottle tops, dominoes, and even Ritz crackers. Well, I was taken with it, anyway. When I finally pulled myself away, the rest of the group had vanished.

As we wandered through the exhibits, spread over three floors, we learned of the gruelling life in the plantations, the harsh sea journeys as seen through the eyes of the slaves, and we followed the journey of rum, sugar and spices back to Whitehaven, where they were eagerly anticipated.

Sugar was the new gold. The British couldn't get enough of it and quickly became known for their 'sweet tooth'. It seems that sugar awakened our predisposition for sweetness; if you've ever tasted mother's milk then you'll know how sweet it is.

We were back in the courtyard now and looking around for our own sweetener – a little tot of rum awaiting us in the gift shop at the end of the tour.

I was tempted to knock mine back sailor style, but common decency prevailed, so delicate sips were the order of the hour. I distracted myself by gazing at the incredible kinetic clock which every half hour springs into action, telling the story of how rum is made, from the harvesting of sugar cane under the Caribbean sun to the bottled rum.

A visit to The Rum Story shop, as well as other stores in the area, reminds you that Cumbrian food was certainly influenced by all that produce coming in from the Caribbean. There's rum butter, ginger and allspice products, and the rich Rum Nicky with its filling of dates, rum and sugar.

We wandered slowly towards Whitehaven Station and for the first time in 14 days we had nothing much to do. No appointments, no hike, no deadlines. I think we both felt a little flat, subdued. It's a bit like the Christmas comedown when there's been all that build up and then it's suddenly over and you're left wondering what to do next.

As I really do love planning, I guess it makes complete sense that once everything is done and dusted, I'll feel a little empty.

I knew, though, that Beth was really looking forward to the coastal journey which lay ahead. As we neared the station, her excitement was infectious, so our spirits lifted and we walked onto the platform as the train approached.

The four of us settled into our seats (by now our backpacks were the size of a small human) and, unwrapping some chocolate, nestled in to enjoy the views.

I checked the route; many of the places were request stops, so not a great deal of demand. We'd be passing through lots of places I'd never heard of — such as the wonderfully named Corkickle — and a few others I had; St Bees, Sellafield, Seascale.

For much of our journey we were just feet from the shoreline, the grey, murky sea rolling in close to the line. Many times the train simply crawled along, giving us ample time to check out the cottages and beach huts right there on the shingle ridge just below the railway.

When we arrived back in Grange-over-Sands, Beth's husband Steve was still out at a county show, so I didn't get to say a proper thank you to our trusty Gin Sherpa. I think here is the perfect place to do it. So — thank you, Steve!

As I loaded my car with the bits and pieces I'd brought with me, I couldn't quite believe it had been almost two weeks since we'd set out from Beth's house. It felt more like I'd driven up for a quick day's hike, done it, and was now off again. What had happened to all that time in between? What a good job I'd made notes and taken photos as evidence!

A five-hour drive lay ahead, so I'd arranged to split it up by dropping into Manchester, my home town.

Manchester: what's not to love? The best music, the best football, the first atom splitting, Coronation Street, the first computer and the best chip barm. *Dead good.*

As my husband never fails to remind me, 'You can take the girl out of Manchester, but you can't take Manchester out of the girl'.

Spirit/liqueur info sheet

Product	Jefferson's 1785 dark rum 40% ABV
Category	Dark rum
Who makes it?	Whitehaven Harbour Commissioners
When did it start production?	The Jefferson's business was founded in 1734 and the production of rum on the family estates in Antigua started in 1785 R & H Jefferson's rum trademark is reputably one of the oldest labels in the United Kingdom
Where is it made?	A blend of Jamaican and Guyana rums expertly blended in Amsterdam to the Jefferson's unique recipe
Key ingredients	A rich, dark rum with a fine balance of deep toffee, liquorice and vanilla with a subtle hint of honeycomb and ripe fruit at the finish
Where can I buy it?	http://www.rumstory.co.uk/shop/
Best way to drink it	Straight, excellent in cocktails or as a mixed drink Or try: **Treacle** 60ml Jefferson's rum 15ml cloudy apple juice Dash of Angostura bitters Tiny drop of sugar to taste Orange zest

Beer info sheet

Brewery	**Unsworth's Yard Brewery**
Who runs it?	Peter Unsworth and Mark Grunnill
When did it start production?	Opened in January 2012
Where is it made?	Unsworth's Yard, Cartmel

The beers

CRUSADER GOLD
Full name: Sir William Marshal's
Crusader Gold
ABV: 4.1%
Style: golden ale
Tasting: lightly hopped, crisp and
refreshing with a subtle citrus
finish
Availability: cask and bottle

CARTMEL PENINSULA
Full name: Cartmel peninsula,
Lancashire, north of the sands
ABV: 3.8% Style:
English bitter
Tasting: mellow with a sweet,
slightly caramel finish
Availability: cask and bottle

SANDPIPER LAGER
Full name: Cartmel Wharf
Sandpiper Lager
ABV: 4.6%
Style: premium lager
Tasting: cold fermented premium
lager with lemon notes
Availability: keg and bottle

COCKLER
Full name: The Flookburgh Cockler
ABV: 5.5%
Style: stout porter
Tasting: packed with dark chocolate
and caramel flavours
Availability: cask and bottle

LAST WOLF
Full name: Sir Edgar Harrington's
Last Wolf
ABV: 4.5%
Style: red-brown ale
Tasting: rich malty bitterness with
red fruits and chocolate notes
Availability: cask and bottle

CARTMEL PALE
Full name: From the Land of
Cartmel – Cartmel Pale
ABV: 3.7%
Style: pale ale
Tasting: sharp, grapefruit finish
built on complex malt flavours
Availability: cask and bottle

CARTMEL THOROUGHBRED
Full name: Cartmel Thoroughbred
ABV: 3.5%
Style: blonde
Tasting: light but full flavoured
with a strong finish
Availability: cask and bottle

Where can I buy it?	Beers are widely available in free-house pubs and high quality restaurants and artisan food shops within the Cartmel and South Lakes areas http://www.unsworthsyard.co.uk/stockists/

Beer info sheet

Brewery	**Keswick Brewing Company**
Who makes it?	Sue Jefferson
When did it start production?	Spring 2006
Where is it made?	Keswick

The beers
Current range of 4 regular cask beers, 7 bottled beers and 1 canned beer plus new K range beers

KESWICK GOLD ABV 3.6%
A golden bitter with a subtle citrus and spicy flavour and aroma

KESWICK BITTER'ABV 3.7%
This chestnut brown ale combines four malts and two English hops giving depth of flavour. A well balanced easy to drink session ale (formally Thirst Session)

THIRST QUENCHER ABV 4.3%
A refreshing Pale Ale with an exotic fruit and citrus aroma. Thirst Quencher uses Maris Otter malt and New Zealand and American hops to create this refreshingly pale beer.

K.S.B. ABV 4.8%
Keswick Special Bitter. A rich malty bitter. Full malt flavours with notes of chocolate and roast barley. Fresh hop aromas (formally Thirst Fall)

DARK HORSE ABV 6%
Rich dark ale made using a combination of five malts and a blend of traditional and spicy hops. A definite must for dark beer lovers

THIRST RUN ABV 4.2%
Golden pale ale with body, subtle malt flavours and using hops giving a citrus note. Well balanced and moreish

THIRST CELEBRATION 7%
Celebrating 19th-century India pale ales, combining three malts and traditional English hops

PARK YOUR THIRST 3.9%
Golden ale with a subtle citrus flavour and aroma. This beer has been created to celebrate 60 years of the National Park Volunteers

CUMBRIAN CHALLENGE 3.6%
Created to celebrate the Cumbrian Challenge and the work of the Walking With The Wounded charity

THE K SERIES consists of 10 new beers created to celebrate the 10th anniversary of Keswick Brewing Company in 2016

K1 – This chocolate brown ale uses generous amounts of chocolate malt and orange peel to give a depth of flavour with English Admiral hops for their citrus orange flavour and aroma. 3.9%

K2 – This pale golden ale showcases English grown Cascade hops with their floral and grapefruit aromas. 3.5%

K3 – This ruby red ale uses American Falconers Flight hops to compliment the rounded crystal and darker malt flavours. 4%

K4 – This New World IPA uses Maris Otter pale ale malt and New Zealand grown Wai-iti hops for bitterness with lemon, lime zest and mandarin notes. 6%

K5 – This cloudy wheat beer uses wheat malt and German Perle hops which give a subtle spicy orange hop flavour. 4%

K6 – This pale ale uses pale ale malt, an American style yeast and American Belma hops which have a subtle strawberry aroma. 4.5%

7K – This amber ale uses amber and crystal malts with English Minstrel hops to give a balanced malt flavour with an orange and spiced berry aroma. 3.8%

K8 – This golden ale uses English Pilot hops for bitterness and is infused with botanicals to create a clean refreshing beer. 3.6%

K9 – This oatmeal stout uses dark malts giving a roasted flavour and English Phoenix hops which give notes of spice, chocolate and molasses. 4%

K10 – This golden ale uses crystal malt and showcases English Archer hops which give notes of peach, apricot and lime. 3.9%

Where can I buy it?

http://keswickbrewery.co.uk/shop

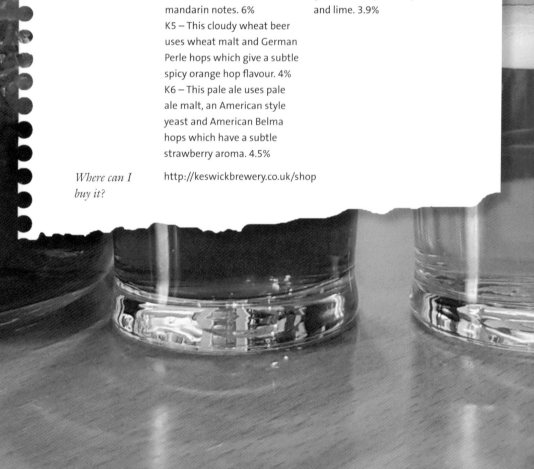

The one that (nearly!) got away

A couple of months after we completed our hike I was in Kendal, perusing the drinks section of a local food stockist (I'm not completely obsessed with drinks and was looking for ideas for Christmas presents, honest I was…) when I spotted a bottle of Damson Gin from a company called Cumbrian Delights based in Staveley Mill Yard, just outside Kendal. How had we missed these? The bottles are gorgeous and, when I looked at their website, I found their range of drinks was imaginative and impressive. I tracked down the owner, Geoff Monkman, and demanded answers.

"Why didn't we spot you before we set out?" I asked.

"Because we only started making the spirits in September 2017," he answered.

Well, that all makes perfect sense. The only problem now was how to sneak them into the book with the publishing deadline fast approaching. I called Karen.

"I've found another local producer that I think we should include," I said.

"Another one? Is there anyone in Cumbria NOT currently brewing their own hooch?"

I looked at the 6 litres of sloe gin I had on the go in the kitchen. "Erm…"

"Well, what do they make?"

"3 gins, 3 vodkas and a rum punch – I've tried a few of them, you know, just to be polite."

"Any good?"

"Mmmmm."

"You're drinking one right now aren't you?"

"Only because I thought that this way we could share the experience."

"What's it like?"

"Divine – the only way I can think of describing it is 'meaty' – properly rich and full of fruit. They started off by accident when they made some fruit syrups for their wedding, and they were so good that all the guests wanted to buy more."

"Any chance of them supplying the shops in Cyprus?"

"Unlikely, but I still think we should include them – they've got a lovely shop in Staveley and Geoff is a really nice bloke – they do pickles and chutneys and jams too, and loads of it is diabetic-friendly and gluten free."

"OK, we can pop them in at the end."

"Perfect."

"Maybe you could save me some to try when I come over the for the launch party?"

"Hahahahahaha – oh wait – were you serious? How about I buy you a bottle to take back with you – deal?"

"Deal."

Epilogue

'Are you going to see each other again?'

I always remember Cilla asking this question at the end of Blind Date, and how most of the contestants squirmed as they tried to say the right thing. It's a question many of my friends have asked and I'm sure you're all asking it too – did we really get on and are we now BFFs?

Well, we definitely got on. Yes, we irritated each other along the way, but we got along brilliantly and shared a lot of laughs and great memories. Karen is all of the lovely things her friends said she was. We are very different, though, which you've probably picked up as you've read the book. Karen hates rain, I really don't mind it. I hate shopping, Karen loves it. Karen loves Gregg's sausage rolls and I can't bring myself to set foot in the shop. I love history and Karen would probably cheerfully batter me with my walking pole if I launched into another one of my 'imagine all the people who have walked this way before us' monologues.

I know we'll remain friends and I'm looking forward to seeing Karen again when she's next in Cumbria, but I'm not sure either of us would describe ourselves as BFFs – plus she's always a million miles away in some exotic corner of the world soaking up the sunshine while I'm happy yomping around the beautiful boggy fells.

I've also kept in touch with some of the people we met along the way too: Andy and Zoe from Shed 1 invited me over to their first birthday party, and Sarah and Stewart at Crumble Cottages are now firm friends. These are people I really wouldn't have met had it not been for my unhealthy obsession with gin and my crazy ideas for walking projects.

Karen

'Did you really get on okay? *Really?*'

My friends and family couldn't wait for me to dish the dirt.

I think I disappointed them. 'We did. Honestly.'

It was just normal; we bickered a bit, got on each other's nerves a bit, scowled a bit. That was as bad as it got. I do think we rubbed along incredibly well together considering we were almost joined at the hip for 12 days, 24 hours a day.

We were good at giving each other space and considering the other's standpoint, even if, on occasion, we couldn't actually agree in the end. We were considerate. I know Beth still feels bad about whipping a crisply battered fish from under my nose in Whitehaven, but all is forgiven. I think she deserves a medal because she didn't touch an egg in any shape or form for the whole two weeks and I know she adores them. She insists it wasn't because of me. But it was. I just know.

The thing is, aside from our beloved writing and hiking (bog off, rain), we have very little in common. The proverbial chalk and cheese. For this trip, it all worked. I had a great time hiking with Beth. You don't always need to have some *thing* in common as much as some *why*.

And perhaps the true test is to find that several weeks later I am looking forward to meeting up with Beth again. Good job really. Because now I can't even pour myself a gin without thinking of her. Now that could've been awkward.

With gratitude and thanks

This adventure really wouldn't have been possible without the help and support of a lot of people – especially the producers who took time out of their hectic schedules to meet with us and tell us their stories and those kindly souls who offered us free (or much reduced) accommodation.

We've mentioned all of them in the book but here are all their websites so you can contact them directly.

Producers

Shed 1 Gin – Ulverston – www.shed1distillery.com
Kin Vodka – Newby Bridge – www.kinvodka.co.uk
Unsworth's Brewery – Cartmel – www.unsworthsyard.co.uk
Gilpins Gin – www.gilpinsgin.com
Cowmire Hall – www.cowmire.co.uk
Kendal Mintcake Liqueur – Kendal – www.kendalmintcakeliqueur. com
Keswick Brewing Company – Keswick – www.keswickbrewery.co.uk
Lakes Distillery – Bassenthwaite – www.lakesdistillery.com
The Rum Story – Whitehaven – www.rumstory.co.uk
Cumbrian Delights – www.lakelandartisan.co.uk

Accommodation

Virginia House – Ulverston – www.virginiahouseulverston.co.uk
Crumble Cottages – Cartmel – www.crumblecottages.co.uk
Kendal Hostel – Kendal – www.kendalhostel.com
Sally's Cottages – Cumbria – www.sallyscottages.co.uk
Armathwaite Hall – Bassenthwaite – www.armathwaite-hall.co.uk

Miscellaneous

Cumbria Crystal – Ulverston – www.cumbriacrystal.com
South Lakes Ecology – www.southlakesecology.co.uk
Hydroflask – www.hydroflask.com
Dodd's Restaurant – Ambleside – www.doddsrestaurant.co.uk
Ginger Bakers – Kendal – www.gingerbakers.co.uk
Herdy – Cumbria – www.herdy.co.uk
Windermere Lake Cruises – www.windermere-lakecruises.co.uk
The Twig Pen People – www.thetwigpenpeople.com
Higginsons of Grange – www.higginsonsofgrange.co.uk

We hope that you obtain considerable enjoyment from this book. Great care has been taken in its preparation, and at the time of going to print all routes follow rights of way or permitted paths. However, roads and the countryside change, diversion orders can be made and permissions withdrawn, and weather and other natural features can vary considerably. Whilst every care has been taken to ensure the accuracy of the route description, the products sampled and places visited, the authors and publishers cannot accept responsibility for errors or omissions, or for changes in the details given.